All Saints *for* All People

All Saints *for* All People

150 years of All Saints, Clifton

John Hudson

First published in 2018 by Redcliffe Press Ltd.
81g Pembroke Road, Bristol BS8 3EA

www.redcliffepress.co.uk
info@redcliffepress.co.uk

ISBN 978-1-911408-34-5

British Library Cataloguing-in-Publication Data
A catalogue record for this book is available from the British Library

text © John Hudson
design and typesetting © Stephen Morris 2018
set in Garamond 12.5/15.5
Printed and bound by Cambrian Printers

Cover picture: The baptistry windows at All Saints, created by John Piper
and inspired by the River of Life and the Tree of Life in Genesis.

Contents

Foreword

All Saints for All People is a book about a church. Well, as you'll read, you'll see it's actually a story of three church buildings over these past 150 years. But more importantly, it's about one church family – the worshippers and community who have found All Saints to be a sacred place meeting the needs of different people over a number of generations. People experience this in different ways. For some it is, and has been, a place of joy and worship, for others refuge and support, or prayer and reflection, or music, learning and art.

Most significant are two truths. 'All Saints the church' is open to all. This was a key aspect of the original foundation when other local churches catered only for the expanding middle and professional classes and to have a seat in church would cost money. From its very beginning All Saints was different. Anyone and everyone was welcome. This is a characteristic the present church, the active worshipping community, continues to embrace. Second, the going out is as important as the coming in. The church building does provide a special and sacred space and place, yet it is in the world in which we live. The Latin liturgy of the mass closes with the words 'ite missa est', translated directly as 'go, it has been sent'. The idea that this conveys is that having attended worship, or prayer, or meditation and reflection we have been 'sent closer to God', and now we are 'sent' out into our world to live our lives as best as we are able, to the benefit of others and of creation.

Enjoy this account, the story of three churches and of one people. Note how All Saints came into being, the work of a group of lay people who recognised a need and responded. Nowadays this would be called a 'church plant'. Read how through a series of trials and tribulations it has flourished and remained true to the original intention of the founders – and it is continually made new for each generation.

Remember that All Saints exists for all people, and it is from this place we are sent into the world to make a positive difference, to the glory of God.

Fr Charles Sutton, Summer, 2018

Vicars of All Saints

1868 Richard William Randall
1892 Henry Bodley Bromby
1911 Maurice Paget Gillson
1939 Cyril Edric Tomkinson
1943 Fabian Menteath Elliot Jackson
1946 Albert Horace Luetchford
1968 John Colin Norton
1981 Jeremy Andrew Younger
1984 Peter George Cobb
2004 Richard Dunstan Hoyal
2014 Kim Taplin
2015 Charles Edwin Sutton

150 years of All Saints, Clifton

A tantalising anniversary, one hundred and fifty years. Such a long time ago, yet there are people in the All Saints, Clifton family who can look back over half of it, and who doubtless in turn remember parishioners who dated from almost the beginning of the story in the late 1860s. What is certain is that whether looking back a century and a half, seventy-five years or a good deal shorter a time than that, there are stirring stories to be told. And without doubt there will be very many more in the years to come.

Two separate issues were the driving forces behind the founding of the church, and both stemmed from matters that had become major preoccupations in the Church of England in mid-Victorian times. One was the growing influence of the High Church Tractarian movement, which had sprung out of Oxford in the 1830s; and the other, inspired to some extent by the Reform Act of 1832, was a feeling that the practice of better-off worshippers reserving and renting pews should play no part in modern church life.

Clifton, of course, was a prestigious address in Bristol, but some of the streets tucked away to the west of Whiteladies Road towards its lower end could be humble enough and in truth, even many of the houses in the grand Georgian terraces farther east had seen better days by the middle years of the nineteenth century. Their glorious reawakening would dawn again but as anyone who is able today to look back even fifty or sixty years can testify, in some cases it was a long time coming.

In 1893 the churchwarden and parish magazine editor Forster McGeachy Alleyne surmised in *All Saints, Clifton*, a book to mark the church's twenty-fifth anniversary, that its story 'will be a living example that even at the close of this practical nineteenth century, a body of ordinary and unpretending people on the outskirts of a busy town and in the centre of what has been contemptuously called "a villa population" thought it worthwhile to erect and maintain a high standard of Catholic worship, and to keep brightly burning the lamp of Catholic Truth.'

Forster Alleyne also touched upon an abiding aspect of All Saints church life when he wrote of the congregation's strong mission to look outwards and help others. Looking back to the earliest days of the parish, he reflected that 'There was an absence of the very poor, so that the constant calls of time and relief were not so pressing as in other parishes.' This meant that demands on its resources in the immediate neighbourhood were not so great that All Saints could not focus on being 'a centre and example of worship'. It also meant that it could look beyond its boundaries to help people in greater need.

The call for the new church did indeed come from lay people living locally, rather than through the diocesan authorities; there was, after all, no shortage of churches in and around Clifton. All of the early figures we look back upon today are men, but any number of women were working just as ardently behind the scenes and leaving it to their husbands and male friends to make the case, as was the way things were done in those days. What is clear is that All Saints' founding fathers, who formed their first committee in 1862 with the express intent of creating a large new church open freely to all, were very much in tune with the radical thinking of their time. The call for an open house church was certainly challenging and new, and as for wishing to build a church in the Catholic tradition, by this time what had started as the Oxford Movement was identifying itself very much as the branch of the church that was at the forefront of preaching the word in a forceful and imaginative way, as well as championing working- (and out-of-working-) class families. The problem, which was soon to come to a head, was that by no means all Anglicans shared an enthusiasm for High Church ritual, and antagonism reached boiling point within a handful of years of All Saints' foundation.

The Anglo-Catholic mission to poorer people stemmed partly from the very basic reason that in some dioceses, bishops opposed to what had come to be known as 'ritualism' assigned the poorest and worst-paid livings to its advocates, the East End of London being a prime example. Maybe it was because of such adverse conditions that priests of this persuasion became known to be among the most fervent and outreaching in the land, while the colour and richness of their ceremonial contrasted irresistibly with the grey and grim world beyond their church walls. For these men and their parishioners in places of heart-aching squalor and depression, 'the beauty of holiness' was a phrase with tangible meaning.

By the 1860s, the figures at the heart of the early Oxford Movement – John Keble, Edward Pusey, John Henry Newman, Henry Manning and their acolytes – were beginning to fade into history, and of course the last two of these had eventually transferred their allegiance to Rome; but the tradition they had re-established so relatively recently was not going to go away in a decade in which the rawness of the emerging communities of the Industrial Revolution had begun to mature into the first traces of the Britain we know today. All over the country public money was being put into schools, parks and open spaces, swimming baths and museums, while 1868, the year of All Saints' consecration, saw several significant steps forward in the way our country saw life. In January the final convict ship from England to Australia reached port, while May saw the last public hanging, when a Fenian bomber was executed outside Newgate Prison. In early June, six days before the All Saints consecration, the first Trades Union Congress was held in Manchester; the working man was beginning to exert his influence.

A further move forward for the 'humbler classes' was the second Reform Act in 1867, Britain's next faltering step along the way to equal voting rights for all adults. It had been brought in by the Conservative government after Westminster politicians had accepted that there was more to be done to iron out shortcomings of the 1832 Act; but it left the country still well short of 'one man, one vote', and remained firmly based around property qualifications. Needless to say, there was no question of voting rights for women.

The most important change, and one that affected the new All Saints parish considerably, was the granting of the vote to urban 'occupiers', men aged twenty-one or over who rented properties, as well as to lodgers who paid rent of £10 a year or more. As a result, the electorate grew from around 1.43 million to almost 2.5 million, but it was still widely accepted that the upper middle classes continued to dominate the scene. It was Lord Derby's government that introduced the 1867 Act but early in 1868 the ailing aristocrat was replaced as Prime Minister by his Chancellor Benjamin Disraeli, and by the end of the year his party had been ousted from power by Gladstone's Liberals. If Disraeli's hope had been that the newly enfranchised lower orders would gratefully sweep his party back into power, he was by no means the last Conservative leader to discover that the electorate can be a perverse bunch. On the other hand, he had always boasted that the 1867 Act had gone much farther in extending the vote than anything the Liberals might have come up with, and maybe this was the aristocrats' and middle classes' chilly verdict on that claim. Whatever, we can conclude that this church was the product of a time of quite significant social change.

A brief summary: at All Saints, the architect George Edmund Street was invited to prepare plans for a church to seat eight hundred people, and its chancel was consecrated on June 8, 1868, with a temporary brick nave attached. Progress was steady and enthusiastic in

The church before the addition of the narthex in 1909. The lower portion of the tower is as it is today, giving us some idea of the great height of George Street's original nave

parts, enough for the lofty and impressive permanent nave, considerably higher than the chancel, to have been added by 1872, but the completion of the tower would have to wait. In all, it is estimated that the church before its later additions cost £35,000 to build and furnish, leaving aside gifts of furniture and decorations, and that money did not come easily. Although price comparisons are always open to question, one estimate tells us that £100 in 1870 was equal to around £11,000 in 2016; do the maths!

The battle faced by the early fund-raisers was graphically summed up in 1865 by a letter to the *Bristol Record* newspaper from a correspondent signing himself Anti-Pew; looking back today, it is easy to admire his zeal while perhaps questioning his skills in making friends and influencing people:

'Sir – It is stated that an anonymous friend has offered a noble sum of £2,000 towards the completion of All Saints Church, on condition that a further amount of £1,300 is raised within a certain time. Will the churchmen of Clifton and Bristol allow any doubt to exist as to the prompt fulfilment of this condition? Most of your readers must know full well what the present Clifton churches are – atrocious monuments of human selfishness, dedicated to St. Dives and the Golden Calf. The description of them written twenty years ago still holds: "You that thirst, come not near the sacred soft-cushioned preserve – vested property, freehold interest, or anything or any term you please, for the privilege which one man pays for, under the invidious pew system, of shutting another out of the House of God. The rich and the non-resident occupy the reserved seats, and those few that are still nominally free are filled by servants, as impatient as their masters of the poor man's contiguity to their lace and livery. Is it not the church of the poor man? He has no business there in that atmosphere of *eau-de-Cologne* and *bouquet-de-la-reine*."

'Is not this witness true? And see more to the same purport, excellently put, in *The Churchgoer*, published at Bristol in 1845. It is only astonishing that any man with a conscience can be found to say a word in favour of such a state of things; and yet I think I remember the incumbent of Holy Trinity, Hotwells, attempting (not very successfully) an apology for the pew system at the last Church Congress.

'Now, the new church of All Saints is to be the first really free and unappropriated church in Clifton, with no private boxes and no reserved seats – a true house of prayer for all people... It will, indeed, be a shame if such a work be allowed to languish for want of funds. I can quite understand the dislike of the Puritanical party to this threatened inroad on their Simeonite preserve; but what I cannot understand is the apathy of many who call themselves High Churchmen, and who yet are content to give little more substantial than good wishes to this great work. Good wishes, however valuable, will never roof in All Saints Church. Men must learn to put their hands into their purses and to give liberally; and it is impossible to blind our eyes to the truth that if all in Clifton and Bristol who profess sympathy with open church principles would come forward as they ought to do, All Saints would be speedily and worthily finished, and there would then, at all events, be one church in that barren and dry land of fashionable selfishness where the poor as well as the rich should have the Gospel preached to them.'

Intemperate words, but Anti-Pew's letter gives us a glimpse into the spirit in which All Saints was founded – the fervent belief that here was a unique gift to the community, not only in its interpretation of the church's mission but in sharing that mission with all who wished to be a part of it, rich or poor. 'St. Dives' was presumably some false god better known to Anti-Pew than to most of us today. As for 'Simeonite', this refers to the fact that the livings of all of the churches in Clifton were (and in some cases still are) in the gift of the Simeon Trust, founded by the evangelical preacher Charles Simeon and sympathisers. The long-time Vicar of Holy Trinity, Cambridge up to his death in 1836, Simeon shared with others a concern that their kind of teaching, which they saw as 'gospel ministry', should flourish in the Church of England, particularly in the light of the perceived threat

13

of the Oxford Movement. They built up a number of ordained followers, but many bishops and private patrons would not appoint them because of their emphasis on personal faith.

This led Simeon and his allies to set about meeting the challenge in a very practical way. Until 1898 advowsons – the right to present a vicar to a parish – were open to be bought and sold like any other commodity, and when in 1812 his banker brother Edward died and left him a legacy of £15,000, he and others set about acquiring parishes for like-minded clerics. He was especially keen to establish 'spheres of influence', clusters where he hoped the impact of his churches would be greater than the sum of their parts. The growing industrial towns of Bradford and Sheffield were fruitful territory – and so were the waning West Country spas of Bath, Cheltenham and Clifton. Today, Simeon's Trust is still responsible for the patronage or a share in more than 160 livings in most English dioceses; and it emphasises that these days, its churches adhere to a wide range of Anglican traditions. Less so in the 1860s, at least in the eyes of the beleaguered proponents of All Saints.

In his book of 1893, Forster Alleyne singled out Thomas Todd Walton, the local secretary of the Society for Promoting Freedom of Public Worship and soon to become one of All Saints' first churchwardens, as a man who 'might almost be called the Church's Founder, so untiringly did he work to promote its building and to collect subscriptions'. Alleyne details various direct three-figure donations made by this benefactor, but also tells an astonishing tale of sheer grit and persistence, which Alleyne considered might strike his late Victorian readers as 'unostentatious... even pathetic': 'Mr. Walton left on his death a small red ledger that noted all the contributions he had collected for the new church, and in the back of it was an almost entire page of the *Clifton Chronicle* that listed all of these in detail.' The page, Alleyne noted, 'was cut up and divided into streets, and almost every dweller therein is marked in some way or other as to his intentions. How patient and untiring must this work have been! How many times must his feet have trod those pavements before he found all the inhabitants at home! And how earnest and how persuasive must his eloquence have been before he drew donations from so many! Neither was he contented with one visit only. There is evidence that both backward and willing subscribers were looked up again and again.'

In fact Thomas Todd Walton was so much in on the birth of the church that it was in his drawing room on November 13, 1862 that he met with four other men in that first formal gathering to discuss creating a church with 'free seating for all and a richer pattern of worship'. The opportunity had arisen because of the rapid population growth in Clifton which had left churches in the city end of the suburb struggling to cope with the crowds on a Sunday. At St. John the Evangelist Church, at the junction of Whiteladies and Apsley Roads, the Revd. H.G. Walsh was so under pressure for space that he was willing to have his parish divided – and knowing that there was a growing call for a free and open church in this part of town, he asked his churchwarden Harrington Bush to explore the possibilities. Mr. Bush was one of the five at the drawing room meeting.

The proposed parish lay between Whiteladies Road and Pembroke Road, with Oakfield Road to the south and to the north, All Saints Road and 'a line drawn to the boundary stone in Whiteladies Road close to where the old turnpike stood'. The first proposed site in the heart of this area fell through, but part of a field in Pembroke Road was made available by the Society of Merchant Venturers, and the drive for funds began in earnest – even though the site did not allow for a literal west-east orientation. It was agreed on April 25, 1863 that George Edmund Street would be appointed as architect, and in July his plans were approved. The first excavations were made in August, 1864, and by November 3 progress had been such that the foundation stone was laid. The ceremony was performed by Sir Alexander Beresford Hope, a writer on the Irish Question in particular and Conservative M.P. for both Maidstone and Cambridge University. 'This is a building in which, if I understand it rightly, religion is not to be folded up and put in a cupboard, like a Sunday set of clothes, to be used only one day in the week,' said the M.P., who was a wealthy benefactor for several Anglo-Catholic projects and a member of the Privy Council. How this fledgling church would grow to fear that it might need a friend in that particular high place before very long.

By the time he was working on All Saints, George Street was in his prime both as a leading architect in the Gothic Revival style and as an authority on medieval Gothic architecture in Europe. His early years in the profession were spent as an assistant to George Gilbert Scott, but in 1849 he set up his own practice in London, and in 1866 had taken on the commission for which he is now best known and which would arguably kill him – the Royal Courts of Justice in the Strand in London. In fact construction on that project did not begin until 1874, so it did not compete for his attention with All Saints to any degree. What was very much on his mind was his almost simultaneous work on the nave of Bristol Cathedral, a major undertaking that brought him to the city frequently for some years.

(To explain the Law Courts' effect on Street's health, he died in 1881 at the age of 57 after suffering a stroke on his walk home from his Surrey village railway station one evening, and many of his friends believed his end had been hastened by the strain of that work.

The building was opened by Queen Victoria in 1882, the year after his death.)

Although most of us are now almost entirely aware of Street's original All Saints solely through photographs and written accounts – and in many cases only with the later addition of the narthex and tower by other hands – we know that over the years it has been widely seen as a more pleasing and successful piece of work than his completion of the cathedral. In his *North Somerset and Bristol* volume of *The Buildings of England*, published in 1958, Sir Nikolaus Pevsner sees the architect's cathedral nave as 'rather dull, though admittedly very earnest'. On the other hand, 'Street's All Saints, Clifton, of 1868 was... a very powerful design'. The German-born Sir Nikolaus then goes on to remind us that English was not the language in which he felt most at ease when he concludes rather bathetically: 'It is a great pity that it was hit by a bomb.' Nice church, shame about the bomb.

At the cathedral, it must be said, Street was restricted in ways he most certainly was not at All Saints; he was being called upon to complete and complement not only a lofty medieval building but, in the chancel, one of the true treasures of fourteenth-century English architecture. His brief was to create a building of equal height to produce a 'hall' church, and his solution was to provide a nave that echoed the feel of the chancel without ever remotely trying to compete with it. Pevsner did recognise this, but concluded: 'After the thrills of the chancel interiors, one tends to be impatient with what is the respectable performance of a sensible architect.'

Writing some fifty years later, in 2010, the late Michael Jenner was more sympathetic towards George Street's cathedral efforts in his book *Bristol's 100 Best Buildings* (published by Redcliffe Press). 'Street's work is often criticised, I think unfairly,' he wrote. 'He continued the chancel's pattern, but with slight variations to ensure that nobody would think that the two were contemporary.'

The first vicar, Richard William Randall, came to All Saints from Lavington, Sussex, where he had been rector – and his Oxford Movement credentials could hardly have been more sound. At Lavington he had succeeded Henry Manning, who had gone on to be Archdeacon of Chichester before joining the Roman Catholic church after his wife had died. 'If I may lay my bones under the sod in Lavington Churchyard with a soul clear before God, all the world could not move me,' he wrote to his sister – but as the second Archbishop of Westminster, and the first Englishman to hold the post, Cardinal Manning eventually found his final resting place in rather more exalted surroundings.

Richard William Randall,
All Saints' inspirational
first vicar

Richard Randall had not, in fact, been the first choice to lead the church. Another Oxford cleric, the Revd. H.W. Sargent, Fellow of Merton College and incumbent of St. John Baptist Church in the city, had been named before All Saints' opening as its 'Perpetual Curate'. Perpetual turned out to be fleeting, however, when ill health prevented him from taking up the post, and from the start, in practical terms, it was Richard Randall at the helm. The Sargent family was deeply rooted in the Oxford Movement, and another member of it, John, had been Rector of Lavington before both Henry Newman and Richard Randall. It was a tight-knit circle, and Randall was very much a part of it.

The fact that he went on to be Dean of Chichester speaks of the high esteem in which he very quickly came to be held, both among his congregation and the higher powers in the church. In 1893, long after he had left All Saints for Chichester, Forster Alleyne wrote:

'In Clifton a quarter of a century ago... the popular conception of a ritualistic priest was a pale, emaciated young man who lighted candles and perhaps put on vestments in the early morning but who... would hardly dare to do so at the orthodox 11 o'clock service, and who could not be expected to show himself in society. In Mr. Randall they found a cultivated English gentleman in the prime of life, full of humour and bonhomie, equally at his ease at talking pleasantly at a dinner party or in making a speech on a platform, entering with as much zest into giving hard hits to an opponent at a meeting as in making the best of speeches at a wedding breakfast. At political gatherings no man was a stronger Conservative, no one a more staunch supporter of the union between Church and State, no one more eloquent against the claims of Rome. Yet this man was a ritualist. There could be no doubt about it, for not only was he vicar of a most beautiful church in the very midst of Clifton, but at the mid-day service costly vestments were worn and gorgeous banners carried in solemn procession...'

We need not infer from this pen-picture that everyone in the congregation shared Richard Randall's taste in politics, but we might surmise that Forster Alleyne, barrister-at-law and scion of a plantation-owning family in Barbados, most probably did. Intriguingly, Alleyne was a graduate of Merton College at a time when the chapel there was a hotbed of the Tractarian drive, so we can conclude that he had very sound Oxford Movement credentials of his own.

Richard Randall's relatively late appointment was not the only change of plan. There is strong evidence that the first proposal was to dedicate the church to the Virgin Mary, but for reasons neither Forster Alleyne nor anyone else has been able to explain, that did not go ahead. Perhaps it was felt that the Bristol area already had sufficient St. Mary's churches including, of course, an extremely high-profile one at Redcliffe. Second-choice site for the church, second-choice incumbent, second-choice name; it might be concluded that in the circumstances, All Saints has not done too badly.

From the beginning there was a daily celebration of the eucharist, with two on Sunday, as well as daily morning and evening prayer. The principal service on Sunday morning was a choral eucharist, presented with the kind of dignity and solemnity that from the start had the church defending itself from its Protestant critics and explaining that all it did was in accordance with the regulations of the Church of England and the desires of the diocesan bishop. Within a few years a choir school was started – one of a good number of private or independent schools in this part of Bristol – and it continued until financial pressures forced its closure in 1962. Thus, for almost the first century of the church's existence, it was possible to offer daily choral services and full 'cathedral music' on Sundays.

The consecration on June 8, 1868 was on a Monday, presumably to allow as many clergy as possible to attend. If this was the plan it was certainly successful, with some seventy of them supporting the Right Revd. Charles Ellicott, the Bishop of Gloucester and Bristol; but the congregation was also full and enthusiastic, as befitted a church that had come about very largely by popular demand.

The next day's *Daily Bristol Times & Mirror* carried a detailed account of the proceedings, recording that the foundation stone had been laid in1864 and the land on which the church was being built formerly belonged to the Society of Merchant Venturers. The reporter was intrigued, as any good newspaperman would have been, by the presence of two unwelcome visitors: 'A short distance from the church, on the other side of the road, were to be seen during the morning two men with billboards, having on them in large letters the words "No Semi-Popery!" From this and various rumours it would seem that an impression prevailed that the services would be of an ultra-ritualistic nature. Such, however, was decidedly not the case yesterday. The service as a whole very much resembled that of the Cathedral.'

The newspaper report suggests that it was not too lengthy an affair. The choir chanted psalms 84, 128 and 132, and the only hymn recorded was 'Blessed City, Heavenly Salem' (A. & M. 243). The first lesson was Genesis 22, 10 to 17, the second Hebrews 10, 19 to 26. The sermon by the bishop – referred to throughout the newspaper report as 'the Lord Bishop' – was based on 1 Corinthians 20, verse 28: 'That God may be all in all.' Afterwards there was a luncheon for some hundred and fifty people in the Drill Hall, without which no seemly Victorian gathering would have been complete.

At this social event, Richard Randall did not hold back on his vision of the course the church should take. As the *Times & Mirror* reported, he said he came to the congregation 'reckoning on their hearty English feeling – more so, on their hearty English Church feeling – determined, with God's blessing, that the faith of the English Church – the old faith of centuries (hear, hear) – dearer to them under a higher name, the old faith of the *Catholic* Church (hear, hear) – should sink deeper and deeper into the heads of those who held it.' Time and again he repeated the phrase 'English Church', reclaiming the High Church tradition as the centre ground of Anglican worship: this was not some recent fad dreamed up by a group of clever men in Oxford, he was implying. This was the very foundation of our faith. The 'hear, hears' told him loudly and clearly that he was preaching to the converted.

The *Church Times* of June 13 carried a rather more pointed article than the local press, born of deeper knowledge of the church politics involved. Happily, it was written by a High Church sympathiser; from another pen it could have painted a very different picture:

'Monday, June 8, 1868 is a day long to be remembered in this very Protestant watering place. "A black day for the Church of England, sir," said a gentleman of "Low views" to a friend of mine. Of course, what he meant was that it was a black day for pewdom and beadledom, for Puritanism and lavender-glovism, for the dear old system of once-a-week services and once-a-month sacraments, in fact for the fashionable religion of Clifton.

'The consecration of a church that is to be free and unappropriated forever is in itself a great event in a place where locked pews for the wealthy and brackets for the poor have hitherto been the rule. The service of consecration was most heartily performed. I thought the Bishop seemed a little perplexed now and then by the ritual – but happily His Lordship does not, like his predecessor Dr. Baring, wish to make his own will law in all the minutiae of ceremonial. It was somewhat ludicrous to see our Worshipful and Radical Chancellor, Mr. Monk M.P., bearing his solitary protest against Ritualism by manfully looking south throughout the Nicene Creed.'

The names dropped in this piece are a reminder of just how much Charles Ellicott stepped out of line when, as anything but a ritualist, he allowed All Saints to go ahead. It would certainly not have happened under his staunchly evangelical predecessor, Charles Baring, or under the man Baring succeeded, the long-serving James Henry Monk. His stance can be gauged by the fact that it was his son, the Liberal Member of Parliament for Gloucester and diocesan chancellor Charles Monk, whose petty protest at the All Saints service was noted with such glee by the *Church Times* correspondent.

The still makeshift church of 1868 waited four months for its first and in fact only wedding of the year, when John Coen married Mary Frances Atkins on October 13. Other than that, marriage licence No. 1 in the archives is perhaps more notable for what it does not tell us than what it does since Richard Randall, for all his outstanding skills and virtues, is no friend to today's family historian or sociologist. His practice was not to disclose any of the grooms' or brides' ages, simply entering 'Full' in the relevant boxes, while for addresses he simply wrote the participants' home parish. Thus 'All Saints' is all we know about where Mr. Coen lived, while Miss Atkins was a stranger from all the way up the hill at Christ Church.

John Coen's occupation appears as 'Gentleman', as is that of his father, another John.

Charles Atkins, father of the bride, is not a 'Gentleman' but an 'Esquire', and it is hard to imagine even the class-conscious Victorians being able to tell one of those from the other in a crowded room. John Coen junior, by the way, has a second Christian name which appears quite illegible to this observer; indeed, Coen itself seems an odd name, and might be something else. Even more frustrating than Mr. Randall's challenging handwriting, however, was his unerring practice of leaving every bride's occupation panel blank. There are even one or two cases where they do seem to have been filled in, only to then be firmly struck through.

The second wedding did not come along until nearly a year later, on August 2, 1869, when Alfred Pope, solicitor, married Mary Ralph. Two comfortably middle-class affairs to set the ball rolling, then, but after that a church determined to bring the gospel to the working man began to show its true colours. Four of the first ten grooms gave their occupation as 'clerk', while a commercial traveller, an umbrella maker, a draper, a mariner and what appears to be a bell-ringer are among the first couple of dozen. In the fourth wedding, in October 1869, Henry Chudleigh married Martha Eggleton: he was a labourer, as were both his and his bride's father, while the space for Martha's work, of course, remains blank. Perhaps she really was a lady of leisure, sitting at home sewing a fine seam, but it hardly seems likely.

The first baptism was on December 13, 1868: Ethel Margaret, daughter of Mary and Joseph Ramsdale, Gentleman, of Stoke Bishop. It was on the following day, however, that we glean a hint of the exciting spirit ushered in by the new priest, since he had the pleasure then of baptising three adults, all doubtless enthused by his teaching. Sarah Davies, Priscilla Dean and John Stephens had committed themselves to God barely six months after the infant church had come into the world.

Forster Alleyne stressed in his book an abiding aspect of All Saints church life – still very much with us today – when he wrote of the congregation's strong mission to look outwards and help others. Looking back to the earliest days of the community, he reflected that 'There was an absence of the very poor, so that the constant calls of time and relief were not so pressing as in other parishes.' This meant that demands for its social work in the immediate neighbourhood were not so great that the church could not focus on being 'a centre and example of worship'. But it also meant that it could look beyond its boundaries to help people in greater need.

Its formal commitment to this work began in 1877, when it resolved to help a new church in Bedminster find its feet, one that started in a tin chapel named Holy Cross in Ashton Gate the following year. Even after it had become a parish church in its own right it continued to enjoy All Saints' support for many years; another church in the Anglo-Catholic tradition, it changed its dedication to St. Francis of Assissi in the 1880s and though it is not unique in the Church of England to go by that name, there are not many of them. By 1887 it was prospering well enough to open one of the biggest suburban churches in Bristol, and All Saints' support played a part in this. Ironically, both the Clifton and Ashton Gate churches perished in the same series of Luftwaffe air-raids in 1940 but St. Francis's had rebuilt by 1953, in a very different style from the new All Saints.

Photographs of the interior of the early All Saints show a chancel behind a not unduly heavy screen – quite delicately proportioned compared with some at the height of the Gothic Revival – and a dominant east window showing Christ in Glory surrounded by His Saints – some seventy saints, in fact, in a riot of detail, colour and exuberance. Responsible for this and all the stained glass in the church, including the teeteringly high clerestory, was the John Hardman company of Birmingham, for many years Augustus Pugin's sole collaborators in this medium. In charge of the project was John Powell, a member of the Hardman family and Pugin's son-in-law.

The sculpted reredos, almost as striking a focal point as the east window, again shows Christ surrounded by saints, this time in the Testimony of the Saints to the Divinity of our Blessed Lord; there were by no means as many of them as in the window but they were nevertheless striking figures, sculpted by James Redfern and gorgeously painted by Daniel Bell and Richard Almond in one of their London-based company's first commissions. All three were still young – Redfern barely thirty, Bell and Almond still in their twenties – but all made an indelible mark on Gothic Revival architecture in Victorian times, and their employment at All Saints is a reminder of the internationally high standards the church's founding fathers set themselves.

Redfern, the son of a Derbyshire mason, worked with George Gilbert Scott on the Albert Memorial, executing the figures of the Virtues, as well as on several cathedrals and Westminster Abbey. Perhaps most imaginatively of all, from around 1873 he collaborated with William Burges on the fantastical mock-medieval decoration of Cardiff Castle, and it is perhaps for this extravaganza that he is most highly regarded today. His efforts in 'restoring' some of England's medieval cathedrals are not universally admired by the purists –

The breathtakingly ornate chancel and altar of the original church, with the reredos depicting the Testimony of the Saints to the Divinity of our Blessed Lord carved by the master James Redfern and gorgeously painted by Daniel Bell and Richard Almond

but even from nineteenth-century photographs we can tell that his reredos at All Saints was an exceptional piece of work for a suburban parish church. On the other hand, other carving in the church was carried out by a sculptor who at the time was even better known than James Redfern – the London artist Thomas Earp, who collaborated with most of the Gothic Revival giants – George Gilbert Scott, George Frederick Bodley, Augustus Pugin and Samuel Sanders Teulon – as well as George Street. He could point to a distinguished reredos of his own, at Exeter Cathedral, but is probably best known for his carving of the 'Eleanor Cross' outside Charing Cross Station in London. It is not the kind of Eleanor Cross the widowed and grief-stricken Edward I would have recognised in the thirteenth century, but as a memorable High Victorian party-piece it has few equals. And here was this sublime sculptor playing a supporting role to Redfern at All Saints, Clifton.

The chancel was flanked by two side chapels, with the organ chamber to the left or (liturgical) north from 1870 and the Lady Chapel on the south side. Of course money had been tight in the early days and for a couple of years the organ had been makeshift, put together partly with sounding boards taken from an instrument that had recently been made redundant by Bath Abbey. The first congregations at All Saints often commented on its sweet sound but it was accepted that in the long run it would not be equal to the high musical standards to which the church aspired, and by 1870 it had moved on to St. John's Church on the corner of Apsley Road.

Its replacement, built by Hill and Sons of London, was a serious improvement, an instrument of great power and pleasing tone. In 1873, very shortly after it was installed, pneumatic action was added to the great and pedal organ sections, and water-driven single-cylinder bellows that were noisy from the start were replaced by double cylinders in 1886. This proved a very satisfactory solution, and soon the eccentricities of the previous system were passing into folklore. 'If the water supply failed, the only way to provide wind for the organ was by hand pumping,' one old-timer recalled. 'A panel of the organ case had to be removed, and two men on a platform some three feet high had to rotate a big wheel. It was an exhausting but exciting operation!' The Hill organ served All Saints well until 1924.

The organist and choirmaster from 1876 to 1921 was Cedric Bucknall, and none of his successors has come near to matching his forty-five years at the fore of the church's music. That said, his successor, William Kirby, served from 1921 until 1948 to be followed by Ernest 'Bill' Fry, who spent thirty years at the console. When Ken Smith arrived in 1978 he well knew that his distinguished predecessors saw their roles as the church's director of music as a long-term project and followed their lead with distinction, staying in the post until 2006.

A particular curiosity in the original church was the presence of two pulpits, the result of George Street, for all his great virtues, not quite getting his acoustics right. His friends swore that this was to some extent down to the fact that the church had been built piece-meal, the permanent nave following the chancel by some years, but the fact remained that the first pulpit, in a phrase never heard in the 1870s, was not fit for purpose. An immediate solution was to bring in from elsewhere in Bristol a battered old wooden structure from which John Wesley had allegedly preached, and by putting it against one of the nave pillars the audibility problem was solved, at least temporarily.

Reading between the lines in Forster Alleyne's early history of All Saints in 1893, there then seems to have been quite lively discussions over what to do next. 'It would have been easy to move the old pulpit to the site of the temporary one,' he wrote, 'but Mr. Randall had imbibed an affection for it in its original position... After fourteen years, however, it became obvious that something must be done. The wooden pulpit, always unsightly and little less than a scandal in contrast to its surroundings, had become crazy, and to an energetic preacher positively unsafe.' In December, 1890, a committee voted to leave the original pulpit where it was and replace Wesley's preaching post with an elaborate new concoction of marble and alabaster, which eventually cost £440. The personnel involved in this are yet another reminder that when it came to adorning their church, only the best was good enough for the All Saints flock. The pulpit was designed by 'Mr. J.L. Pearson, R.A. (who since Mr. Street's lamented death has acted as architectural adviser to the Church)' while the contract for the densely detailed carving of the alabaster went to Nathaniel Hitch.

Both these figures were prominent in later Gothic Revival. The prolific John Loughborough Pearson is perhaps best known for his brilliant twin-towered west end at Truro Cathedral, which makes his somewhat prosaic west end at Bristol Cathedral a disappointment to some critics. He also designed the reredos at Truro – with Nathaniel Hitch its sculptor. Today we can again only marvel at the prestige as well as the skills of the craftsmen who created the early All Saints, Clifton.

In 1992, one or two older members of the congregation were able to recall the original, pre-war All Saints of their childhood. 'It was very dark,' said Father John Bunker-Morley. 'Not frighteningly dark, but mysteriously dark. I can remember once when Father Cyril Tomkinson was standing in the nave, and an elderly lady arrived early for high mass. She was going down the side aisle quite quietly in order to take her place. Father Tomkinson said: "You there, sit down, sit down. I'm

THE PANELS OF THE NEW PULPIT.

A detail of the intricate carving on J.L. Pearson's elaborate pulpit of 1891, the work of the sculptor Nathaniel Hitch

preaching." The old lady was frightened to death. The normal way into the church then was through the narthex, now St. Richard's chapel, but you could also come in through the tower, as we do today.'

When Rosemary Bird was a child in pre-war days, she recalled that there would be a servants' mass, allowing them to be back at their houses in time for work at 7 a.m.; then the 'gentry' would go to the 8 a.m. service. More remarkable by far, though, was her explanation of the seating arrangements: 'The women would sit on the left and the men on the right. This had nothing to do with the sound of the singing, but to make sure the men wouldn't eye up the women but concentrate on singing. Couples who insisted on sitting with each other had to sit on the left side aisle. These chairs were known as "the sheep and goats".'

Mrs. Bird's theory on the reason for the segregation policy would probably not bear close scrutiny, but it did happen, and what perhaps seems most odd about it today is that all this came about in a church that prided itself on its free-and-easy attitude to seating arrangements!

Christopher Verity, still a server into 2018 though impaired by ill health in recent times, has two memories of the old church, though he confesses that they are not very detailed. Born in 1935, his earliest recollection is of his brother's baptism in 1939 and the second, when he was five, is of his being a tassel boy in a service some three weeks before the bombing in 1940. He officially started serving in the sanctuary seventy-five years before 2018 at Corpus Christi, 1943, when he was eight. But three years before that he was dragooned in when one of the tassel boys did not turn up one day, making him one of extremely few living people to have served at a service in George Street's church. 'I wish I could tell you more about it,' he laughs. 'The fact is, I didn't know what I was doing. All I knew was that there was bags of noise and bags of smoke and a very big man carrying a very big banner.' Tassel boy, boat boy, torchbearer, acolyte, crucifer, thurifer, master of ceremonies: Mr. Verity is one of those men who has performed every duty in his long, long service to All Saints.

Back in the early years, the men with placards at the consecration of the chancel were as nothing compared with what was soon to come. From the start, local opposition to the All Saints way of doing things seems to have created what might be seen as almost a siege mentality among some members of the congregation. Before very long it would prove to be amply justified, but at first the more sanguine argued that quite possibly the antagonism towards the church was not quite as threatening as some supposed; after all, it was thirty years on from the beginnings of the Oxford Movement, and by now the High Church tradition was scarcely unknown and disregarded. Then again, when opposition did rear its head there was always someone close to All Saints to fight the church's corner. Maybe it was always Anti-Pew by any other name. Whatever, it was a Ritualist who rose to the bait when somebody calling himself Presbyter Anglicanus – literally 'Anglican Priest' – had written disobligingly about All Saints in the *Bristol Record*.

'I would remind him that there are parties in the Church of England holding opinions very wide apart,' a Ritualist wrote. 'All Saints Church, Clifton was built by Ritualists, for Ritualists, and is supported by a Ritualist congregation who worship there in the enjoyment of their own warm and hearty services. I can only say that if Presbyter Anglicanus objects to the services at All Saints, there are plenty of Low churches in the city. I can assure him that he will find plenty of room in them if he does not find a seat which, I believe, are kept very exclusive. All Saints is always crowded with its own congregation, and the attendance of Presbyter Anglicanus at a church more in accordance with his own ideas will doubtless be endured.

'The fact is, we Ritualists (for I am proud to avow myself one) are not yet understood. The letter of Presbyter Anglicanus is simply a type of popular feeling. It is thought sensible to decry Ritualism. Let it be so; we can go on our own way, waiting for the time when people will see a deeper meaning in what appears to them mere external show.

'I cannot close... without pointing out in the letter of Presbyter Anglicanus an affectation of ignorance for the gratification of a sneer. I allude to that portion of his letter where he describes the celebrant as wearing "something like a white shawl". One so familiar with Roman ceremonial as he professes to be must have been perfectly aware that the priest referred to was vested in a chasuble, also worn by the clergy of the Roman Church.'

All good knockabout fun, but in the 1870s the debate grew significantly more dark and sinister, to the extent that some feared that all the diligent work of the Oxford Movement in transforming worship in the Anglican church for all who wished to see it transformed would be wiped away in little more than a generation. The Archbishop of Canterbury since 1868 had been Archibald Campbell Tait, son of Scottish Presbyterians and indeed the first Scot to hold that office. As a former headmaster of Rugby School – succeeding Thomas Arnold – and Bishop of London, he was the kind of able and authoritarian figure Queen Victoria wished to see upholding a strictly Protestant Church of England, and on April

20, 1874 he introduced a parliamentary private member's bill that sent shock waves through many more churches than All Saints, Clifton.

Within four months his Public Worship Regulation Bill had become law, gaining royal assent on August 7, 1874. The Conservative government had fast-tracked it by giving it its backing, Prime Minister Benjamin Disraeli calling it 'a bill to put down ritualism'; the practices of the Oxford Movement, he opined, were no more than 'a mass in masquerade'. The Liberal leader William Gladstone, on the other hand, was enraged. As a High Church Anglican who favoured the separation of church and state, he was appalled by the thought of the liturgy being turned into 'a parliamentary football'. He and many others were equally distressed when the new act established a court to hear grievances presided over by a former divorce court judge, Lord Penzance; not only was there parliamentary interference with worship, but now it would be supervised by a secular court.

The Act struck many as a witch-hunt. It allowed an archdeacon, a churchwarden or any three adult male parishioners to notify their bishop if in their opinion there had been any alteration or addition to the church fabric, ornaments or furniture without lawful authority; that the incumbent had worn any unlawful ornamentation, or failed to use any approved wear; or that the priest had strayed from the directions set down in the Book of Common Prayer. The bishop had the discretion to stay proceedings but if he allowed them to go ahead, the accusers were obliged to accept his decision with no right of appeal. If they did not agree, then the matter would be sent for trial.

Between 1877 and 1882 five clergy were imprisoned for contempt of court, two from London and one each from Liverpool, Manchester and the West Midlands. The first, and therefore the most highly publicised, was the Revd. Arthur Tooth of Hatcham in East London, that High Church hotbed. At All Saints, Richard Randall must have followed his case with something more pressing than interest. Tooth had been appointed to the working-class parish in 1868, and his efforts to renew the life of his church started to attract large congregations. His approach combined capable preaching, ritualist practices and various parish organisations to help needy residents.

The new Act gave a group who disapproved of his ritualism the chance to have him charged with, among other things, the use of incense, vestments and altar candles. In truth, it was not for this that he was imprisoned, but his refusal to attend and recognise the authority of the court, after which he continued to ignore both the judicial warnings resulting

Richard Randall as he is portrayed in his window in the narthex. Above him, George Street's original church is shown with an imposing spire – which never did get built

from his non-attendance and various legal attempts to prevent him from exercising his ministry. He was in gaol only briefly, but the disruption that followed his arrest and imprisonment was key to bringing the Public Worship Regulation Act into disrepute, not least when his conviction was quashed on a technicality. He continued to work within the church, but never again took charge of a parish.

Prosecutions ended in 1906 when a Royal Commission recognised the legitimacy of pluralism in worship, but astonishingly, the Act remained in force for ninety-one years, until it was repealed on March 1, 1965 by the Ecclesiastical Jurisdiction Measure of 1963.

The plain fact was that Richard Randall was going through all this at much the same time that Arthur Tooth was suffering, except in his case it did not lead to court hearings, less still imprisonment. Nevertheless, these were unpleasant and unsettling times. As we know from the men with placards at the consecration in 1868, there had been clamorous opposition to the All Saints way of worship from the start, but this rose considerably in volume at around the time the mighty new nave was opened on August 8, 1872, not least because visiting preachers that day including two prominent High Church bishops in George Moberly of Salisbury and 'Honest John' Mackarness of Oxford.

Two months before the ceremony clerical opponents in Clfton sent a 'memorial' challenging All Saints' practices to that long-suffering Bishop of Gloucester and Bristol, Charles Ellicott, who gave them some encouragement by saying that while he did not feel Richard Randall could be charged with any breach of the law, 'I do not disguise my regret that usages – some of which appear certainly to be contrary to the law as recently laid down in the court of the Archbishop and by the Privy Council – are complained of as practised at All Saints, Clifton.'

Bishop Ellicott's delaying tactic was to tell the complainants that if they wished to take up the matter with his court, in which he would be the sole judge, then they were invited to do so. In the meantime: 'After long and careful consideration, I have come to the conclusion not to withdraw the licence from existing curates, such a course seeming to me hard and ungenerous.' Instead, he proposed to lay down conditions for future clergy at All Saints and to renew his offer of a bishop's court hearing, the expense to be borne by the memorialists. In April, 1873, they replied somewhat tetchily: 'The memorialists feel that they have done their part in calling the attention of the Bishop to notorious and flagrant violation of the law, and they respectfully decline to share with him the duty which they contend belongs to him alone.'

And there the matter might well have rested until Archbishop Tait's Public Worship Regulation Act came along. On October 13, 1876, Bishop Ellicott's registrar received a complaint against Father Randall under the act which was put forward by three complainants, Edward Davies, William Henry Gregory and Robert Henderson. The matters complained of in the first memorial and repeated here look ludicrous today as a possible cause for litigation: the wearing of vestments, altar lights, making the sign of the cross, and administering communion as a separate service. What is more, the complainants were concerned 'that as the beginning and a part of the rite and ceremony of public worship, the clergy and choristers entered the church singing and in a procession, preceded by a man wearing a surplice and holding aloft a large cross, and on their entrance into the chancel all bowed before or towards a large cross standing, or appearing to stand, on the altar...'

Charles Ellicott was a serious theologian and academic, and he simply had no wish to be involved in any of this, as he told the memorialists in complex and legalistic terms; and that was the end of that. Nevertheless, in establishing his neutrality he felt it politic to distance himself from All Saints, to the great sadness of both Father Randall and the congregation, and between 1873 and 1889 he declined to license clergy to the church. After that he showed his firm support for life in the parish, holding annual confirmations there whereas previously candidates from All Saints had had to go to St. Mary Redcliffe. The (temporarily) final coming in from the cold came in 1891, when Richard Randall was appointed an honorary canon of Bristol Cathedral.

In late Edwardian times, All Saints began to catch up with building work that had been in the minds of the congregation for some time. 'Then there is our church, near and dear to us all,' Forster Alleyne wrote in his history twenty-five years on from the consecration. 'A generation has passed by since it was built. Our fathers raised it from the ground and beautified it at a cost of £35,000. Are their sons going to do nothing? He outlined various possible steps forward, and among his suggestions he wrote: 'We want a Porch to the Church to protect ourselves from draughts, and to form a place where we may inscribe memorials to those departed ones whom we long to commemorate: can we not build it?'

Like many developments in the church it did not come easily, but ten years after that plea plans were finally beginning to fall into place and in 1909 work was at last complete. By this time it had transformed from a porch to a narthex, a narrow entrance hall at the west end of the church, though accessed, in All Saints' case, from the liturgical north (though in real life west!) side. 'Narthex' is a rather grand word, and for some people there is almost a sense of bathos in the discovery that it means nothing more than a vestibule; it should surely be something more holy than that? In fact the origin of the word is arguably more down-to-earth still. It comes, through Latin, from the Greek for the giant fennel plant, with its long, hollow stem. Obviously some imaginative souls in the early church thought there must have been a resemblance but even where narthexes survive in their original form today, you rarely hear talk of Mediterranean herbs on churchgoers' lips.

Now renamed the chapel of St. Richard of Chichester and reserved as a quiet place for private prayer – arguably the precise opposite of its original purpose – the narthex was designed from the start as a memorial to Richard Randall and also to the parents of the second vicar, Henry Bromby, who came to All Saints in 1892. By great good fortune – or maybe something more – the three windows on the geographical north side of Street's building were left intact by the bombing, and today they give us a glimpse of the reverence in which the first vicar and some of his early contacts in the church were held.

Each depicts three luminaries who preached at least once or in several cases multiple times from 1869 until the year of Father Randall's departure in an annual cycle of sermons known

THE REV. HENRY BODLEY BROMBY, M.A.,
PRESENT VICAR OF ALL SAINTS'.

Henry Bodley Bromby was All Saints' second vicar, from 1892 to 1911. He was related to the prominent Gothic Revival architect George Frederick Bodley, who designed the narthex completed in 1909

as the octaves. This refers to a period of eight days beginning on a feast day, and in this church it was the patronal All Saints' day and the subsequent week. It is an impressive group – too late for the founding fathers of the Oxford Movement to be involved but including many of the leading Anglo-Catholics of their day; besides, at least John Keble

150 YEARS OF ALL SAINTS CLIFTON

and Edward Pusey from the early days are not forgotten, as their stained glass images, rescued from the bombed church, have been incorporated into the doors of a wall cupboard in the chapel.

The left-hand window shows the American-born William Newbolt, who preached at All Saints in 1873 as Vicar of Dymock in Gloucestershire but went on to become head of Ely Theological College and later a canon of St. Paul's Cathedral; Edward King, who preached in 1870 as principal of Cuddesdon Theological College but very soon went on to be Regius Professor of Pastoral Theology at Oxford and a founder of St. Stephen's House theological college and finally Bishop of Lincoln, where he battled constantly with the anti-ritual lobby. A close friend of Pusey, he was a pall-bearer at his funeral. The third figure in this first window is George Body, who spoke at the first octave in 1869 when he was vicar of the soon-to-be-consecrated Christ Church in Wolverhampton and was to become one of the leading Anglo-Catholics in the Midlands. He preached at many octaves right through to the last one of this first cycle in 1892 and was one of Richard Randall's most loyal support- ers in the venture.

Featured in the central window are Henry Parry Liddon, who was the first speaker at the first octave in 1869 – subject 'Christ the Giver of Sanctity' – and in the following year was appointed Professor of the Exegesis of Holy Scripture at Oxford, where he did much to restore the influence of Tractarian thinking after a Protestant backlash. He was also made a canon of St. Paul's Cathedral in 1870, and his preaching there attracted vast crowds of up to four thousand. Indeed, he was such a celebrated figure that an 1876 caricature of him in the topical magazine *Vanity Fair*, titled 'High Church', was quite enough to identify him for a largely metropolitan readership. The middle figure in this second window, and therefore the central one of all nine, is Richard Randall, while on his left is Thomas T. Carter, rector of Clewer in Windsor and the third speaker at the pioneering 1869 octave.

In the third window is Richard Meux Benson, the founder in 1866 of the Society of St. John the Evangelist, the first religious order of monks in the Anglican communion since the Reformation. Stemming from a district of Oxford they are still widely known as the Cowley Fathers, even though their base is now in Massachusetts. Father Benson was the third of those celebrated in the narthex windows to have been among the first half-dozen speakers at the inaugural octave of 1869, and he featured several more times in the future.

In the centre of this third group is Edward White Benson, the first Bishop of Truro and a founder of the cathedral there, who was elevated to Archbishop of Canterbury in 1883. He spoke at the 1879 octave on 'Communion in the Faith of the Church' and is probably best remembered for devising the Festival of Nine Lessons with Carols. It was first used in Truro Cathedral on Christmas Eve, 1880, but it must be said that it has been considerably revised since then. The final figure of the nine is Henry Montagu Villiers, who spoke as vicar of St. Paul's, Knightsbridge in 1882 and over several subsequent years. His namesake father had been Bishop of both Carlisle and Durham, but the priest commemorated here lived very much in the milieu of one whose forebears included the first Duke of Buckingham and Barbara Villiers, Duchess of Cleveland, who had five children by Charles II. A prebendary of St. Paul's Cathedral, this Villiers was twice married, first to Lady Victoria, daughter of Lord John Russell and then to Louisa Emily, granddaughter of both Earl Cadogan and the Marquess of Anglesey. This is a colourful window in more ways than one.

That Richard Randall was well worthy of being counted among this august band is made clear in *Kilvert's Diary*, one of the most engaging social histories of Victorian times. Francis Kilvert was a young Herefordshire country clergyman who lived from 1840 to 1879, and the published diaries covering the last ten years of his life are a treasure-trove of gossip, simple optimism, generosity of spirit and the quirky reflections of an inquiring mind. There is also a suspicion that his wife censored them – like his fellow cleric Charles Lutwidge Dodgson (Lewis Carroll), Francis took an innocent but heartfelt delight in the company of very young women – but Mrs. Kilvert had no need for her blue pencil when it came to his report on a national Church Congress held in Bath in the 1870s:

'There was a band, tea, coffee, ices, champagne cup, claret cup, sandwiches, and speeches by the Bishop of Peterborough, the Bishop of Manchester, the Rector of Bath, and Mr. Randall, Vicar of All Saints, Clifton. It was stated that the Bath Congress was the most successful and the largest Church Congress yet held, 1,400 more tickets having been sold than last year at Leeds. Altogether between 6,000 and 7,000 tickets were sold.' Since those tickets cost a hefty 7s. 6d. (37.5p.) that was quite a turnout.

The other significant window in St. Richard's Chapel is in the east wall, a modern piece installed when the church was restored and the for many years redundant narthex was transformed. The ceiling was also extensively repaired and repainted at this time and forms a striking counterpoint to the bare stone walls, very much in the design and calligraphy tradition of the early twentieth century. This window of 1967 was designed by Christopher Webb, his last commission before he had died at the age of eighty in the previous year.

Most of his life's work was in the Gothic tradition; he was greatly influenced by Ninian Comper, who in turn had been an assistant to Bodley, and Webb's early windows might well have been created a century earlier. For All Saints, though, he applied a more free hand, and one with some pleasant touches very specific to the church and its people.

True, in the widespread tradition of churches of this dedication, the main theme is Christ in glory surrounded by saints. But St. John the Evangelist is a reminder of the parish from which All Saints was originally created, the cross held by St. Helena acknowledges the part played in church life over many years of the Men's Guild of the Holy Cross, and St. Wulfstan of Worcester brings to mind the diocese in which Bristol was originally sited; not that it ever was in All Saints' lifetime, of course.

A far more quirky and personal reference appears to the bottom of the window, where Canon Albert Luetchford, the priest who saw the 1960s restoration through to completion, peers out on to the tranquil scene. He is the only figure in the chapel who is still within the living memory of a fair number of parishioners, and it will be a sad day when that is no longer the case. The window was financed in part by a legacy from Ella Madeline Hodgson, whose very significant role in the church's story will be discussed in due course.

Upholding the church's tradition of turning to only the finest in the land to design and adorn its building, All Saints called upon another towering name in the Gothic Revival pantheon, George Frederick Bodley, for its narthex. Surely not *the* George Frederick Bodley, who had been born in 1827, only three years after George Street, architect of the original church in 1868? This *must* have been a later and lesser George Frederick? Not so. There was only one Bodley, and the designer who broke through in the 1850s was still active right up until his death in 1907. It is clear that the narthex at All Saints was one of his final projects, and of course he had died before its opening in 1909.

Not that this was by any means his most bizarrely posthumous piece of work. In 1903 he was one of the assessors for the competition to design Liverpool's Anglican cathedral, and the winner was Giles Gilbert Scott, a twenty-two-year-old prodigy from that famous dynasty. Bodley was appointed to oversee the early construction work in the following year, and was most influential in the design of the Lady Chapel, the first part of the cathedral to be completed. It is noticeably more elaborate than the rest of the building, and it is fair to assume that had Bodley lived longer, it is unlikely that a maturing Scott, with his twentieth-century slant on Gothic, would have kept him on the team. His relationship with the old man was always stormy, and after Bodley's death he submitted an entirely new design for the remaining, major part of the cathedral. Nevertheless, the fact remains that George Bodley, active from the 1850s, played some part in the design of a building not completed until 1978.

August, 1914, is now one of the most ominous months in British history, the beginning of more than four years of the most brutal hostility the world had ever seen. But you would not have known it from that month's All Saints parish magazine. 'Holidaymaking is in the air, and August sees its climax...' the lead story began; not that this was the only monthly publication, by a long way, to have been overtaken and overwhelmed by the turn of events.

Come September the reality was all too apparent, but in his vicar's letter Maurice Gillson's was a calm, feet-on-the-ground and always practical voice, with no place for vainglorious patriotism. 'It is needless to remind you of the unprecedented experiences in which we suddenly found ourselves during August, and which are likely to remain with us for some time to come,' he wrote. 'Experiences which will surely live in our memories for the rest of our lives. What is of immediate importance is that we should play our part each day in such a way that we may not be ashamed when we look back on it in the future, and that we may emerge from this visitation purified and strengthened.'

Father Gillson laid out firm guidelines on what could and could not be done in the indeterminate time ahead. He was clear in mapping out a programme of daily prayer and intercession, while 'the work amongst those who are threatened with poverty through the war is only beginning, and will certainly grow and make large demands upon those who have time to help. This will involve not only the investigation of cases of distress but the befriending of wives and families of our soldiers and sailors by those who will take them their weekly allowance.' What the vicar clearly did not foresee at this early stage of the war was the casualties that would devastate almost every community in the land, and the demands these would make on his flock. What he did add was a plea to leave any first aid work on the domestic front to the Bristol Red Cross Society, and not go in for any independent heroics: 'We must be on hand to do whatever (the Red Cross) needs.'

Even now, however, there was time for other considerations, as was made clear by churchwarden Meyrick Heath in that same parish magazine of September, 1914: 'We see occasional strangers oblivious of our rule against taking our seats during the reading of the lessons and whilst the rest of the congregation is kneeling. If the offenders have long

ceased to be strangers, our feelings are more akin to those of annoyance and amazement...'
War? What war?

Four or more long, tragic years after his pragmatic call to arms, Father Gillson was equally
phlegmatic in his address in the parish magazine of December 1918, a month after the
armistice. 'Reconstruction,' he wrote. 'The word has been before us day by day for months
past, and the many problems which gather round it are liable to tax our elder statesmen
for long enough to come. One aspect of the necessary reconstruction has not been dealt
with in the papers, and it is for us, perhaps, the most pressing one at the moment. There
must be reconstruction in prayer, as in other things.

'The war called forth new energies of prayer throughout the country, and there was a very
wonderful response to that call from many at All Saints. Never shall we forget that faithful
watch of prayer that was kept day by day, winter and summer, through four and a half
years. It has shown what we can do in the way of prayer, and I do hope those energies of
prayer will be carried on and used in other directions... I think many of us will feel that we
cannot go back to the old plan of closing the church at six o'clock. I hope to be able to
keep the church open daily until 8 p.m., at any rate, and on Saturday until 9 p.m.' Once
again Father Gillson was concentrating on the possible rather than the fanciful.

When Forster Alleyne was writing about future building projects for the original church in
1893, as well as the 'porch' that turned out to be the narthex he turned his attention to the
tower, which had never been completed through lack of funds. The architect George
Street's dream had been for a prominent spire, but whatever the solution might eventually
turn out to be, Alleyne saw it as a challenge to be addressed without delay. 'The foundations
of the Tower are laid,' he wrote. 'Can we not complete it?'

Some thirty years later, come the early 1920s, the congregation's answer was yes, it probably
could. Not that the fund-raisers had been idle in the years in between, of course, with
Bodley's narthex, completed in 1909, having proved no straightforward task. These were
substantial architectural projects, and the way All Saints went about their building, only what
the parochial church council deemed the best was good enough. By now, of course, the
princes of high Victorian Gothic revival had long departed; even the engagement of Bodley
some twenty years earlier had seemed scarcely credible to some. But of course there were
other able practitioners working in their wake, and Frederick Charles Eden (1864-1944) an
assistant of both William Butterfield and George Frederick Bodley, was one of them.

Frederick Charles Eden's solution to the completion of the tower in the 1920s, a lead-covered lantern rather than the spire George Street would have favoured

He also trained with the prestigious textile designers Fairfax Blomfield Wade, acquiring skills that would stand him in good stead in another of his specialities, stained glass design. He built only three churches in his career, and a colonial cathedral in the then Tanganyika, while All Saints is one of his two significant urban commissions, the other being St. Matthew, Bethnal Green, which by sad coincidence was also bombed. By far the greater part of his busy career was in church restoration and stained glass, especially after he opened his own studio in 1909. Eden was also curator of the ecclesiastical furnishings display at the British Empire Exhibition at Wembley in 1924; and this was the man All Saints chose to complete its tower, as well as design its war memorial and splendid sacristy.

As we have noted, Street had wished to see the tower completed by a spire, a factor that came to bear in the design of the rebuilt church in the 1960s. Instead, the vote in the 1920s went to a lead-covered lantern or cupola effect, which immediately became 'the pepper pot' to many. It was certainly striking, more urban Flemish than suburban Bristol, and once again it told the world that this was a church that did and saw things differently.

As an aside, the loftiness of Street's original nave is hinted at in a postcard of the church published shortly after the completion of the tower in 1928. In this, the original lower

The church in the early 1930s, a dominant presence in a still almost deserted Pembroke Road

section of the tower, the part that survives today, is dwarfed by the nave roof, while it now more than holds its own with the 1960s structure. However, only its spire gives it its predominant presence today – and if Street had had his way, that would have applied equally to the original building.

As well as the completion of the tower, 1924 also brought the dedication of a new organ, Father Gillson performing the ceremony at evensong on March 24. It was the gift of the recently widowed Monica Wills, the wife of Henry Wills of the tobacco dynasty, in the year before she became a Dame of the British Empire for her charitable work. This time the builders were Harrison and Harrison of Durham and London; they worked in close co-operation with the church organist, William E. Kirby, and on the following day he gave a varied recital that ranged from Bach, Parry and Mozart to two living composers, Edwin Lemare and the South Gloucestershire-born Basil Harwood. The organ was a more subtle and complex piece of work than its predecessor – tuned to the new French pitch, the congregation was told, though few, if any, ever got their head around that one; none of which counted for anything, of course, when the Luftwaffe came calling on December 2, 1940.

From November 24, 1940 to April 11, 1941 there were six major German bombing raids on Bristol; December 2, 1940, the one that destroyed All Saints Church in an incendiary firestorm, was the second of them, and coming only eight days after the first, it told residents that their city was firmly in the Nazis' firing line. Until the raids began there had been a feeling that Bristol was somehow tucked away from the main action, an attitude typified by the BBC, which transferred many of its prime radio programmes from Broadcasting House to Whiteladies Road. These included Tommy Handley's cult comedy show *ITMA*, and for a brief while All Saints parishioners shared the streets of Clifton with such unlikely characters as Colonel Chinstrap, Mona Lott, Ali Oop and the shady German special agent Funf. Nights like December 2 quickly persuaded the BBC that its stars would be a great deal safer in Bangor, North Wales; with the aeroplane company up at Filton, the city docks and major road and rail links to all points of the compass, it is hard to see how the southern city of Bristol could ever have been seen as anything but a likely target in the first place. More than 200 people were killed in the November 24 raid, in which 148 bombers dropped around 12,000 incendiaries and 160 tonnes of high-explosive bombs. That was the raid

The crucifix group that crowns the war memorial in the church grounds. Its architect in the 1920s was F.C. Eden, who also designed the tower completion and the sacristy

that devastated Park Street and the old city area that is now Castle Park, with the Jacobean St. Peter's Hospital and the much-loved timber-framed Dutch House destroyed. Five churches – St. Peter's, St. Nicholas, St. Mary-le-Port, Temple and St. James's – were also badly hit. The Lord Mayor, Alderman Thomas Underwood, mourned the City of Churches that 'had in one night become the City of Ruins'.

It was misty on the evening of December 2, which arguably made what was to come all the more terrifying. True, seeing wave upon wave of enemy aircraft – some 120, in this case – bearing down upon one's home must have been horrifying, but hearing them above the clouds while the bombs hailed down apparently out of thin air surely held its own particular terror. The raid went on from just after six o'clock to 10.30 p.m., when mercifully the prospect of fog over the English Channel and France sent the Germans home rather earlier than they might have gone.

Before they left they had dropped 121 tonnes of high explosives, a tonne of weighty oil bombs and 22,140 of the far smaller and lighter incendiaries, the nemesis of All Saints. The heavy cloud cover meant that their accuracy was awry, to the extent that they missed almost all of their prime targets; no moonlight on the River Avon pointing the way unerringly to the heart of the city that night. The downside to this, of course, was that the bombs fell randomly over a wide area mainly to the north of the centre, with the largely residential areas of Redfield, St. Paul's, Cotham, Redland and Clifton bearing the brunt. In fact Clifton was the first to be hit, with parachute flares and incendiary bombs doubtless meant for the city docks wreaking havoc in its blameless streets and avenues.

For the second time in little over a week the raiders seemingly had the skies above the city almost to themselves. The poor weather meant that no RAF fighters were sent up to join in the fray, while ground-based anti-aircraft guns recorded not a single hit, despite more than 4,500 rounds being fired. On the ground it was the fire service that bore the brunt, with 197 reported blazes fought by a total of 409 pumps and 1,518 men, two of whom died. The overwhelmed city brigade put out a call for reinforcements just before 7 o'clock in the evening and a staggering 63 other forces answered the call, some from as far afield as Oxfordshire, Berkshire, Buckinghamshire and South Wales. Shortly before daybreak the fires were all under control – but for the parishioners of All Saints, and thousands of other residents, that was of little comfort. In all, 156 Bristolians died that night, and a further 270 were injured; and after December 2, everyone knew that from now on, not even the most peaceful of suburbs could feel safe from harm.

41

Between the November 25 and December 2 raids there was a significant change in newspaper censorship rules. The headline in the *Bristol Evening Post* for the first one was 'Germans Concentrate On West Town', for the second 'Nurses' Heroism In Bristol'. As the bombing raids had spread over much of England, increasing numbers of local newspaper editors and their proprietors had complained about the meaningless restriction of only hinting at the whereabouts of the damage. 'It's as if they think Old Jerry is going to look at the *Post* and say "Gosh, it was Bristol we hit last night. We thought it was Stoke-on-Trent",' one veteran reporter complained.

That having been said, newspapers were still constrained to be extremely sparing in detail. For instance, there was not a word the following day about the destruction of All Saints. The Children's Hospital was bombed for the second time in eight days, and the *Post* led on a positive story of uncowed heroism, with doctors and nurses carrying every last one of their young patients to safety. It was, the paper declared, 'one of the shining incidents of the night's events'. For its overview of the dreadful proceedings, however, it had to rely on the bland account put out by the Air Ministry and the Ministry of Home Security:

'Shortly after dark enemy bombers attacked the town. The attack continued on a somewhat heavy scale until a little before midnight. A number of fires were started and considerable damage was done to houses and commercial buildings. Some persons were killed and others injured, but according to reports so far received the number is not large.' Not large, 156 dead, 270 injured? If the authorities had put out a similar statement after the Grenfell Tower fire of 2017, there would have been protest marches through the streets. But these, in more ways than we can possibly imagine today, were very different times.

Apart from its relatively positive story about the Children's Hospital, the *Post* restricted itself to accounts of two separate incidents, the bombing of the Bishop's Palace in Redland and a night at the Bristol Hippodrome that remains to this day part of that theatre's folklore.

In the first, the reporter could scarcely contain his excitement: 'One of the first buildings to go up in flames was a well-known church leader's house. Catching fire at one end it burned right through, flames leaping to a great height. As it burned it presented a remarkable picture, looking like a giant "set piece" in a mammoth fireworks display, its outlines black against the violent blaze... The owner was away from home.'

And then there was the Hippodrome story, though of course the theatre could not be named:

'A variety performance carried on despite the bombs, which fell almost all round it. One high explosive fell outside the front entrance and people sheltering there threw themselves on the floor to avoid falling masonry and glass. At the conclusion of the performance the audience and artistes crowded together in the corridor and the time was passed in community singing led by the band under the tin-hatted, evening-dressed conductor. Solo items were sung by a woman singer who did a very great deal to keep the minds of the people off the happenings outside... A Scots soldier rendered famous national airs in a broad dialect.'

The show was *It's A Funny Thing*, on tour after a popular summer season in Blackpool, with the *Happidrome* radio comedian Harry Korris and the larger-than-life Tessie O'Shea top of the bill. Those in the know would have recognised instantly that this was the Hippodrome through the description of the 'evening-dressed conductor', as the immaculate Sydney 'Don't Call Me Syd' Phasey was one of the city's best-known personalities of the day. If Tessie O'Shea really was the 'woman singer', it is a wonder she did not sue the *Evening Post* for selling her short. But then again, there was a war on.

The most serious incident of the night was at Dean Street, St. Paul's, where a large-calibre bomb had fallen, destroying several three-storey Georgian houses including an air raid wardens' post. Rescuers found the street blocked by heaps of debris and a deep crater, and although twelve people were rescued alive, it took almost a month to recover the bodies of the forty who died; fifteen of those were air raid wardens. In all, the six raids over some eighteen months made Bristol the fifth most heavily bombed city in the country, with 1,299 people killed and 1,303 seriously injured. An astonishing 89,080 buildings were damaged, with 81,830 houses completely destroyed and more than three thousand left fit only for demolition.

It goes without saying that memories of the bombing stayed vivid among church members who were close to it for the rest of their lives. Fifty-two years later, in 1992, when All Saints was celebrating the 25th anniversary of the consecration of the new building, a small group of young people aged between 11 and 15 interviewed a number of them, and the hard work put in by Katie Anderson, Helene and Sarah Badman, Katie Harding, Charlotte and Hannah Hopkins and Barnaby Smith has made a lasting contribution to the recorded history of the church.

Father John Morley-Bunker remembered that his family lived in Pembroke Road, and an incendiary bomb fell in their back garden on the same night: 'Then we saw the church alight. It's said that Father Cyril Tomkinson was having a meal when they knocked on the

December 2, 1940, the most dramatic and devastating night in All Saints' history

door and said: "Father, the church is burning down." "Well," he said, "I must finish my meal first," rather like Sir Francis Drake and his game of bowls. But I understand he did many things, and saved many things from the church.'

Future churchwarden George Ford was on duty in the city with the Civil Defence that dreadful night, and came home dog-tired to find the church in ruins. He was told that incendiary bombs had blocked firewatchers' way out on to the roof, and by the time fire-fighters arrived the blaze was out of control. Mary Densham's memories were very different: 'I had my first baby shortly before we were very badly blitzed. We thought we weren't going to survive, so I got my mother to carry out a kind of baptism on her. As soon as we could after the bombing we had the baby received into the church, and she was baptised in the ruins.'

Arthur Miles recalled that a priority for some early on the scene was the rescue of altar furnishings and the large calvary now to be found in a niche behind the organ. 'We owe their preservation to the boys of Clifton College and their masters, who were able to carry them away to safety,' he said.

Particularly poignant among the parishioners' reminiscences was Katy Anderson's interview with Gordon Lishman, who first started attending All Saints when he was eight years old. Over the years he progressed from a tassel boy to boat boy, while a spell as an acolyte followed before he became a thurifer, and later crucifer. Mr. Lishman, then, was no casual member of the congregation, but it was not until he returned from Army service that the full horror of December 2, 1940 hit him. Standing beside the ruins on Pembroke Road, he simply cried; he could not believe that the church that had meant so much to him for so long was no more.

The Right Revd. Mervyn Stockwood, the high-profile Bishop of Southwark whose Anglo-Catholicism stemmed firmly from his childhood and early adulthood as a member of the All Saints congregation, was another who saw the horror of December 2, 1940 at first hand, as he reflected in his address at the consecration of the new church in 1967. 'The church had an extraordinary hold on us,' he recalled. 'It evoked a strange love and a deep loyalty as it pointed us in worship to the reality of God and the mysteries of the Catholic faith.

'Then came 1940. I was in Bristol on the night of the disaster. It so happened that on the following evening Father Tomkinson had asked me to supper. I shall never forget the two of us standing in the smouldering ruin, the smell of burnt wood, the water, the devastation. It seemed impossible that such a fate could have overtaken our beloved All Saints. But as I look back I see there was a lesson to be learnt. Perhaps we had become too dependent upon a building...'

As would happen in any church in any time in history, adversity only served to bring the congregation closer together. Groups gathered in the vicarage and other houses in a way that pleasingly reminded some people of the early church, and of course even in the chaos of those first few days after the Bristol blitz, among the outpourings of sympathy came some practical offers of help.

The most substantial came from Emmanuel Church, close to Clifton College on Guthrie Road. Surely this was predictable: a fellow Christian congregation, indeed a fellow Church

The church after the bombing. This picture hints at why some people thought it might be possible to rebuild from the ruins

of England congregation, what could be more natural? In fact the proposal was seen from the start as unexpectedly generous but sadly impractical as anything other than a short-term stop-gap. Emmanuel asked their visitors not to burn incense, with its lingering aroma, and as the All Saints congregation understandably wished life to go on as normally as humanly possible, this was a problem. The answer for a while was to celebrate 11a.m. mass in the chapel at Clifton College, yet another neo-Gothic place of worship from the 1860s at which the All Saints flock hoped it could feel more at home.

An odd time-warp: when Emmanuel Church was made redundant in the mid-1970s any thought of its migrating to All Saints was quickly abandoned. The church was demolished in 1977 to make way for more than 60 flats for elderly people, the building following quite closely the shape and roof pitch of the original. Pleasingly, the architect John Norton's 108-foot tower was left standing, still overlooking the scene of Sir Henry Newbolt's 'breathless hush in the Close tonight'.

The move to the college chapel gave All Saints welcome breathing space to think about its future, and its answer was to turn to its parish hall, the Randall Room. For a year or so its conversion was a work in progress but by August 1941 it was ready for use, with everyone lending a hand, including the boys at the choir school. By Easter, 1945 the adjacent sacristy was combined into the body of the makeshift church, with steps leading up to it; and by the time the ciborium designed by the architect William Randoll Blacking for the eventual new church had been introduced late in 1952, some felt that the hall was beginning to feel ever more like a permanent home.

With at least the temporary future of the church secured, in 1943 an exhausted Father Tomkinson stepped down to make way for Fabian Jackson, a priest of some sixteen years' standing whose two previous parishes had been in the London area. He took to the Clifton experience cheerfully enough, but was scarcely at All Saints long enough to make his mark, since in 1946 he left to be Bishop of Trinidad. That appointment, too, was short-term, since three years later he returned to Britain to be rector of Batcombe, between Frome and Shepton Mallet. There he stayed until his retirement in 1967, and he died nine years later. As for All Saints, if it was stability the church needed after so short an incumbency, it certainly found it in Albert Luetchford, whose stay lasted from 1946 right through until the centenary year of 1968.

For the first five years of the 'Little Church', as the Randall Room was coming to be thought of, the choir was accompanied by William Kirby on grand piano, sometimes augmented by a small orchestral group. This changed in 1946 when a two-manual organ made by Rushworth and Draper was installed in an upper gallery, but it was clearly a stop-gap instrument, unfit for any new church to be built in the future. Apart from that, unaccompanied work by the choir called upon the organist to hurry down the steps to conduct and then move smartly up again for the next hymn. But then again, hadn't there just been a war on?

For the organ in the projected new building, as it was being discussed in the late 1940s, the church turned again to the makers Harrison and Harrison, with a contract signed on St. Stephen's Day, 1950. In 1952 the temporary instrument was sold to Queen's College, Taunton, to be replaced by a two-manual organ with a detached console, created in a manner that opened the way to its being incorporated into a more comprehensive instrument when Randoll Blacking's church eventually came to fruition. Crucially, in the short term, the console was now sited beside the choir stalls to cut out those troublesome stairs.

By this time Edward 'Bill' Fry had become organist and choirmaster, and he was doubtless well aware of the organ's limitations; nevertheless he put on an ambitious recital to launch the new instrument, with the *Toccata* from Widor's Fifth Symphony a rousing grand finale. Of course we now know that plans for the expanded organ crumbled when Randoll Blacking's proposals came to nothing as the years passed by, and nobody could have been

The parish hall in Victorian times, decades before it was called upon to serve as the temporary church

more pleased than Bill Fry. 'Having had more experience of organ planning, he now realised how unimaginative and dull this instrument would have sounded,' Tim Stanley reflected in *The Clifton Sound*, a meticulously compiled booklet published to celebrate the launch of the new church's instrument. The Harrison and Harrison organ eventually found its way to the William Temple Memorial Church in the south Manchester suburbs, and for the last two years the Little Church made do with a Positif, a mini-organ loaned by Walker's, who had won the contract for the impressive instrument to adorn the rebuilt church.

In 1992 parishioner Arthur Miles recalled that two of the larger ante-rooms of the converted parish hall became the vestry and sacristy, while there were already cloakrooms and a kitchen in situ. 'We soon settled down and the Little Church served us well,' he said. 'To meet seating demands there were two masses on Sunday. The first was at 9.30 a.m., a children's mass with a 'conductor' who was either one of the assistant priests or a senior server, and this was followed by the 11 a.m. service.

The Little Church in its early days, before the ciborium canopy that graces today's church gave it added presence and dignity

Also in that round of interviews in 1992, Father John Morley-Bunker explained that his memory of what became the Little Church stretched back to 1932, when he first went to Sunday school there. 'I can't say I learned very much at Sunday school,' he confessed. 'The one thing that sticks out in my mind is that there was a kind of upper gallery, from which we used to hurl hassocks down at one another. We also had some rather nice parties at Christmas, when people used to hide sweets under chairs and we would find them.

'In the upstairs there was a little room where we used to belong to a thing called the Coral League. We would colour in letters to be sent out to missionaries in Central Africa; they were written in Swahili so that the children out there could read them. Later on that room became the blessed sacrament chapel in the temporary church.'

Looking back to the early 1950s, Tim Stanley recalls: 'As young children my brother and I attended the earlier Sunday mass with our parents, and the conductor – often Philip Bird – would give what was, in effect, a running commentary on what was happening. That was how we learned about the mass. There was no rolling about on a rug in those days! How pleased I was that after years of suggestions, a family service was very successfully reintroduced by Father Richard Hoyal.'

Arthur Miles remembered that services were well attended, 'and as we still had the choir school, the standard of music for which All Saints was noted was fully maintained. Evensong was sung daily and the choir also sang at the festivals which fell during the week. The anniversary of the consecration of the old church was observed each year by a procession from the Little Church to the ruins. There was then a short service there – with due care taken to keep clear of the main walls, which we were told were unsafe.'

An immediate and unfortunate side-effect of the conversion, of course, was that it deprived the congregation of its space for social activities. Not for nothing, however, are the wartime and early post-war years remembered for their lively community spirit, and the church's social events committee and groups such as the men's society and Mothers' Union branch worked wonders to help keep the parish together. In summer the church garden saw more activity than it had done for years, while the loan of other parish rooms made for some memorable winter journeys, particularly in the wartime blackout years.

So it was that from 1941, throughout the 1950s and well into the 1960s, All Saints kept its head above water next door in Alma Vale Road, in a building hardly designed for High Church worship. The parish hall had served its flock well; now, with social provision very much in mind in the new church complex, it was time to bid it goodbye. Nevertheless, many older parishioners still smile wistfully and think back to happy times when they pass the Garden Court apartments alongside the church in Alma Vale Road.

A highspot of the immediate post-war years was the celebration of the old church's 80th anniversary in June, 1948. Eightieth anniversaries rarely attract much attention, but as the seventy-fifth birthday was in 1943, it is not hard to see why the thanksgiving and fun were put on hold for another five years. On the precise anniversary, Tuesday June 8, high mass in the morning, the Bishop of Malmesbury presiding, was followed in the evening by a social event in the church garden (tickets 2s. 6d., in marquee if wet).

Two days later came show time – 'A Programme of Plays and Music', put on by the Bristol Workers' Educational Association Players and (for the 'music, magic and mirth') Mr. Bertram Luton and Friends. The three one-act plays were all by popular dramatists of the middle years of the last century, and sounded to promise a few laughs along the way. First came *One Evening at Nero's*, by A.J. Talbot, set in 'Nero's study in his summer palace at Baia!'. Talbot tended to specialise in this kind of knockabout, and his *Lucrezia Borgia's Little Party* was another of his sure-fire hits.

Next, when audience members had composed themselves after choir member and am-dram enthusiast Bertie Luton and his pals' antics, came *Woman's Intuition*, by R.J. McGregor, a two-hander with Phyllis Macklin as She and Bernard Tighe as He. And to wind up the evening on a high note came V.C. Clinton Baddeley's *Winsome Winnie*, with Diana May as Winifred and other characters including Lawyer Bonehead, the Marquis of Frogwater and the Marchioness of Muddlenut. It sounds to have been a good night!

Saturday, June 12 brought a further high mass, this time conducted by the former All Saints vicar Fabian Jackson, now briefly Bishop of Trinidad, who was paying a flying visit back home before returning permanently the following year. By this time Christopher Verity was thirteen years old, and events of that day made an indelible impression on him. 'I owe Fabian Jackson quite a lot,' he says. 'When he came back to All Saints that Saturday to preside at mass, he conducted it in such a way that ever since I have taken a keen interest in church liturgy.'

A fete in the church garden started at the usual kind of time of 3 p.m., with 'Stalls, Sideshows, Entertainment, Teas', but it took on a continental air by continuing with dancing under fairy lights right through until 10.30 p.m. The next day, of course, was the usual busy Sunday. The celebrations proved to be a successful fund-raiser, with 'All proceeds during the week for the All Saints Rebuilding Fund, which is in urgent need of further support'. The fact that it would be all but twenty years before these efforts bore fruit is a timely reminder that as in the 1860s, the congregation of the immediate post-war years was a faithful, persistent and patient group of people.

Even before the war ended there were active plans to rebuild the church. An appeal was launched in December, 1943, with some generous donations and legacies setting the fund-raising under way, though nobody under-estimated the enormity of the task. William Randoll Blacking, the Salisbury and later Guildford-based architect who designed the ciborium that remains a potent focal point to this day, was called upon to draw up plans for the restoration, and in 1947 he put forward a proposal that would keep largely to the original building's floor plan and incorporate as much of the existing masonry as possible. He was a designer who specialised in harmonising new structures with old, and was perhaps stronger on individual architectural features than large-scale buildings, that imposing ciborium being a case in point. His plans were approved with enthusiasm by both the parochial church council and the Bristol Diocesan Advisory Committee.

Then, in 1953, came a major setback: the diocese revealed a proposal not to rebuild All Saints but to unite it with the parishes of Emmanuel and St. Mary, Tyndall's Park, with the new grouping to be known as All Saints but Emmanuel the parish church. Not surprisingly this caused a good deal of dismay, not least because of the contrasting traditions of All Saints and Emmanuel, and the rest of the 1950s and beyond were spent in agonised discussion of the way ahead.

In 1959 a new Bishop of Bristol, Oliver Tomkins, succeeded Arthur Cockin, but any hopes that he would overturn the decision were quickly dashed. Father Luetchford was as disappointed as anybody, but he felt bound not to challenge his bishop's decision. Some in the congregation felt the same way, while others accepted that, on balance, the diocese was taking the only practical course open to it in these austere times; after all, there were other churches in Clifton and there was a strong case for war damage reparation funds to be spent on new outreach on the housing estates springing up all around the city, particularly to the south. Nevertheless, there remained a group who felt rebuilding was essential: All Saints had a particular identity, it served a special need, and its loss would be felt in the diocese far beyond the confines of Clifton.

Perhaps not surprisingly, it was Father Luetchford and his followers who won the day, and on June 9, 1958, the parochial church council at All Saints voted against appealing to the judicial committee of the Privy Council, the highest court of appeal for the Church of England in this country. A month later, the Emmanuel P.C.C. made the opposite decision and declared itself eager to appeal – and at much the same time a determined elderly member of All Saints' P.C.C., Miss Ella Madeline Hodgson, struck out on her own and did likewise, not without the support of others in the congregation. Her case was adjourned when the court praised her efforts but asked why her P.C.C. was not represented, a move that hit the ball back firmly into that body's court. Many years later members of the P.C.C. at that time recalled some difficult meetings, one of which went on for so long that the chairman, Father Luetchford, left everybody to it, saying he had to get up early for mass the next day. The Privy Council opened the hearing of Miss Hodgson's appeal in June, 1959 – and more than six months later, in January 1960, the P.C.C. opted to throw its weight behind it. The second hearing of the Privy Council opened on February 20, 1961, and the next month, on March 27, the court announced its verdict: the appeal was upheld, and All Saints was free to rebuild.

In order to secure vital war damage reparation funds, a condition was that the new church should cover the same area as the original one. The old church was large and, of course, traditional in design, and by now, the plans drawn up by William Randoll Blacking in 1947 were beginning to feel out of step with the times. Just how out of step would be made plain soon enough down Pembroke Road, when the new Roman Catholic Clifton Cathedral began to take shape. Another development, in 1958, had been the death of Randoll Blacking, and some time before the Privy Council's decision the P.C.C. had been in discussions with his younger partner in practice in Salisbury, Robert Potter. The day after the Privy Council had given the green light, he was commissioned to draw up new plans.

Like his erstwhile partner he was intrigued by the synergy between art and architecture, both in his work and that of others, and by the time he came to All Saints he was building a distinguished career. From the mid-1950s he had been working closely with Dean Walter Hussey on the renovation of Chichester Cathedral, where they called upon such internationally acclaimed artists as Graham Sutherland, Marc Chagall, John Piper and the sculptor Geoffrey Clarke. He also helped to revive the craft of medieval stonework by setting up a masons' workshop at the cathedral, and when local stone proved less than durable he arranged for supplies to be brought in from over the Channel in Caen. Some years after his All Saints commission he became surveyor to the fabric of St. Paul's Cathedral, creating a treasury in the vaults to display the Wren masterpiece's valuable artefacts. In fact the sympathetic conversion of the vaults of ancient buildings became one of his specialities.

On July 10, 1961 he confirmed to the All Saints rebuilding committee what everybody well knew – that the walls of the original structure were now unfit and unusable. 'Keep away from those walls' had long been the warning to boys at the choir school and other young members of the congregation. Those deteriorating remains are well remembered by congregation member Tim Stanley, who says: 'It was as a chorister at the choir school that I first processed into the ruins. Every year the undergrowth pushing up through what remained of the floor seemed bigger and bushier – a far cry from pre-war days, when I had been told that the huge church was so full for mass on Sundays that some members of the congregation had to sit on the pulpit steps.'

The sanctuary: Randoll Blacking designed the ciborium over the altar for the church he did not live to build, but it harmonises pleasingly with his younger partner Robert Potter's design

As we well know, Robert Potter favoured a radically new direction, and he was delighted when, on September 26, 1961, the P.C.C. unanimously accepted his vision. That said, there was naturally fine tuning to be done and it was not until July, 1963 that his revised proposals were accepted – and then again, there were still adjustments to be made. Potter, as usual planning every last detail, had put forward the idea of a hanging pyx, a form of tabernacle suspended over the altar to hold the sacrament. These had been general through England, Scotland and France during the Middle Ages, but were now so rare that one of the last ones still in use, dating from medieval times, had been destroyed when St. Peter's Church in the old heart of Bristol (and now a poignant ruin in Castle Park) had been bombed in the November 24 raid of 1940.

To have revived the tradition would have been a retrograde step, a consistory court in the Bristol Cathedral Chapter House decreed on appeal, and the proposal was rejected in August, 1964. A curiosity: the chancellor of the diocese who was central to the decision was the brother-in-law of Philip Bird, the churchwarden who was appealing. He did, however, allow the church's appeal against an earlier rejection of holy water stoops, and plans for these went ahead, along with an aumbry in place of the pyx.

By this time the new church's foundation stone had already been laid for nearly a year, C. Cyril Clarke having performed the ceremony amid the ruins of the old church in the previous November, following a blessing by the Archdeacon of Bristol. Mr. Clarke, who by this time was living in the splendid Gatcombe Court in Flax Bourton, was a significant figure

The Blessed Virgin Mary presides over a quiet corner of the church much prized for its air of peace and meditation

in the business and social life of Bristol in the middle years of the last century – a leading light in the Worshipful Company of Soapmakers, master of the Society of Merchant Venturers, chairman of Bristol Hospitals, president of Colston Research Society, chairman of Colston's School governors and much more besides. More to the point, he had been a faithful member of All Saints, Clifton for decades, serving on the P.C.C. from 1920 to the 1950s as well as performing wider church duties, including serving as treasurer of the first Anglo-Catholic Congress in London in the early 1920s.

All well and good, but even *more* to the point – and surely the clinching factor in his being chosen to perform the ceremony – there he stood before all on November 2, 1963, on the decidedly Swinging Sixties day when Gerry and the Pacemakers were knocking the Beatles' 'She Loves You' off the top of the charts, the only man at the ceremony who could point out his name in Forster Alleyne's long-ago All Saints history of 1893. Sure enough, there he is, Cyril Clarke, one of ten 'Boys' at the bottom of a far longer 'List of Servers, Acolytes Etc'. (Apropos of absolutely nothing, one of his young colleagues was a poor little chap called B. Quick. We can only imagine the heavy-handed Victorian jibes that must daily have come his way.)

A wide-angle lens in the balcony highlights Robert Potter's dramatic concept for All Saints' interior

It was Robert Potter's masterstroke to interpret the precondition that the church must cover the same area as the original in a less literal way than Randoll Blacking had. Most members of the congregation, not least Miss Hodgson, had naturally foreseen and indeed wished for a building growing up from the original foundations, and that was very close to what the earlier architect was going to deliver. Potter, however, was a step ahead, and through seeing the plot of land on which the church was built as a blank canvas, with his only remaining points of reference the tower, the narthex and the sacristy, he set about turning these traditional structures into memorable counterpoints to his strictly mid-twentieth-century building. Particularly telling was his recognition that there was no longer a need for a great, conventional nave to seat eight hundred, freeing him to achieve the neat little public relations coup of creating a place of worship where east really was east and west west, rather than south and north.

Over and above all that, however, was the happy chance that in the years between Randoll Blacking's original proposal and the fruition of All Saints' rebuilding dream, there had been a radical rethinking of liturgical needs. The call now, epitomised by the Second Vatican Council of the early 1960s (and Clifton Cathedral) but heeded beyond the Roman Catholic Church, was for the altar to be brought forward into the congregation so that the People of God surrounded it on at least three sides. It was on foundations very divergent from Street's original layout that work began in earnest in October, 1964.

Robert Potter's vision for his new project combined simplicity with focal points of intense colour and, if not always beauty, then at least striking imagery. Central to this were the windows and the vivid hues they could bring to the building, and Potter felt he knew just the artist to deliver his dream. In his work with Dean Hussey at Chichester Cathedral, one of the great modern gems they had introduced was a window by Marc Chagall. Nice thought, but at a parish church in Bristol? Not a chance, no doubt to the relief of the fund-raising committee and its treasurer. On the other hand, another artist of high repute there had been John Piper, who produced a tapestry to illuminate the dark area around the high altar, a blaze of colour with an abstract rendition of the Holy Trinity flanked by the Elements and the Evangelists. Almost inevitably, the press hated it; but Potter and Dean Hussey did not, and Piper's work in this field led him to create further tapestries for Hereford and Llandaff Cathedrals.

It was his growing reputation as a stained glass artist, however, that brought him to Potter's mind at All Saints; that, and the fact that at Chichester the two men had struck up a cordial working relationship. Piper's breakthrough had come when, with his Dutch collaborator Patrick Reyntiens carrying out the practical work, he designed the baptistry window for Sir Basil Spence's high-profile restoration of Coventry Cathedral, a project that for many years was seen as a symbol of Britain's ascent from the ashes of the blitz. The pair were also responsible for the towering lights of the 'lantern' at Liverpool's Roman Catholic Cathedral, that awkwardly distinctive circular structure that makes the building 'Paddy's Wigwam' in the eyes of more irreverent citizens, both pro and con. Piper's whole purpose, of course, was to adorn the interior of the building, and that his work at Liverpool does memorably, with carpets of red, blue and gold light bathing the white marble altar and each of the nine side chapels as the sun revolves around the 'crown of thorns' on high.

Basil Spence at Coventry had laid down the marker for striking and thought-provoking windows in modern church architecture – as did the master builders in medieval times, though with a very different approach – and down the road from All Saints at Clifton Cathedral, the Percy Thomas Partnership was entering into that spirit by planning to welcome worshippers and visitors in its narthex with the brilliant coloured glass fantasies of Henry Haig.

John Piper was noted for his proficiency in many fields, but up until this time he had won most acclaim as a war artist in the 1939-45 conflict, chronicling the blitzed ruins of churches and other public buildings in a way that seemed to give them defiant nobility while never lapsing into sentimentality or jingoism. He spent only a few hours in Bristol very shortly after the air raid of November 24, 1940, but the paintings he produced there – of the ruined Temple Church, Holy Nativity and St. Mary-le-Port – are seen as some of his most memorable. The last is particularly highly regarded, with the still glowing embers through the gaping windows seen by many as a beacon of faith and hope.

As the war progressed he was commissioned to produce a series of paintings of prized historic buildings that had not been damaged but were seen as in the line of fire. In turn, this led several owners of stately homes to call him in and portray their grand houses, and in 1942 the King himself summoned him to Windsor to create a series of watercolours of the Castle and Great Park. It was of course at a time when Piper was still largely immersed in ruined churches, and George VI, who didn't know much about art but knew what he liked, was not moved by the dark, ominous tone of several of the resulting images. 'You seem to have very bad luck with your weather, Mr. Piper,' he murmured drily.

By the time Robert Potter was summoning him to Pembroke Road all this was receding into Piper's past, and although it is for his war images that he will be best remembered in the future, by now he was well known to an even wider audience for his collaboration with the poets John Betjeman and Geoffrey Grigson on the popular *Shell Guides to Britain*. In other words, he was one of those artists that a lot of people had heard of, and his involvement at All Saints was rightly seen as quite a coup.

Baptistry windows had emerged as significant features of recent church architecture, and so it proved with Potter's plan for this church, with Piper's interpretation of Revelation 22's 'sinuous golden form of the River of Life' and 'the Tree of Life with its branches curving upwards, studded with red and gold fruit' dominating the scene; indeed, it is now seen by many as the church's emblem, its brand logo, widely reproduced on postcards, pin badges and promotional material, and is presented as 'a recognised National Treasure'. It is certainly a significant reason why the church was awarded Grade II Listing in 1969 (a ranking renewed in 2001).

Very different in artistic style but a massive presence above the Lady chapel on the south side is Piper's interpretation of the first lines of Genesis, the opening words of the Bible: 'In the beginning God created the heavens and the earth...' In abstract shades and textures of blue, this makes an impact that prompts some to see it as a force of nature, rather than a work of art – especially, naturally, when the sun is shining. Narrow columns of red reaching the full height of the building, along with other incidental adornments, complete Piper's considerable impact on the church interior.

It was on September 26, 1962 that the All Saints P.C.C. approved Robert Potter's suggestion that John Piper should be approached, and around eighteen months later the artist came to Bristol to discuss his thoughts with Father Luetchford. The Diocesan Advisory Council in Bristol was 'unconvinced' by his early suggestions, but gave its approval after some comings and goings. Doubtless some of the early reservations stemmed from Piper's proposal to use a revolutionary (in this field) new medium – fibreglass – painted with coloured polyester resins; but the simplicity of the imagery, especially in the Tree of Life, struck some critics as unworthy of the setting. From the weighty creations in stained glass of the Gothic Revival's finest to a lollipop tree a child might have painted: it was scarcely progress, was it?

The All Saints P.C.C. open-mindedly accepted what Potter and Piper had in mind, trusting the judgment of these two thorough professionals. As for the fibreglass and resin, Piper described the process as being somewhat like painting in situ on canvas, creating large sections without the use of leads. 'There is a prejudice against (this technique) at present,' he explained. 'It is thought to look too synthetic or "plastic", at any rate for churches, but as good artists use the medium more and more, there is no doubt that it will gain ground. In view of the richness of colour and variety, there is no doubt quite a future for it.' Unhappily, he was wrong in this judgment. He remained almost alone in his enthusiasm for fibreglass in this context and though he used the technique again at a church near Reading, All Saints remains far and away his most significant work in this medium.

The problem is that fibreglass is not stable. It expands and contracts according to the weather – sun and rain, heat and cold – and this constant movement can lead to cracking. Over and above that, the coloured resin can slip down from its original planned dimensions,

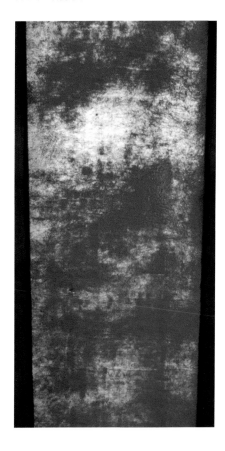

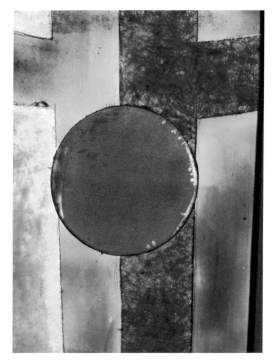

Left and above: Details from John Piper's windows of fibreglass painted with coloured polyester resins – a revolutionary but short-lived technique

Piper's overwhelming Creation window on the south side of the church, which on bright days bathes the interior in blue

and though that is not of urgent significance at this time, it is a consideration for the not-so-distant future. At present, it must be said, no unprejudiced onlooker would view the baptistry windows with any feeling other than this is still very much as Piper conceived them. As for that spacious firmament on high, the great blue south window, any movement of colour could surely be interpreted by some as nothing less than God's plan.

Already some observers feel there is something 'alive' about the windows. They rustle gently and easily on the ear in sunlight and the present incumbent, Father Charles Sutton, has been asked by visitors about 'the sound of running water'. In that this has been in the baptistry, with its simple but substantial Portland stone font and River of Life, this on one level is rather touchingly pleasing, while not being what anyone with any nitty-gritty responsibility for the upkeep of the church and its assets would wish to hear. All that can be said is the issue is being closely monitored, but there is no immediate threat from any possible point of view. As for the future, viable means of stabilisation will doubtless be explored and there is every confidence that the Piper windows will be enhancing the church for a very long time to come.

The organ is another striking feature aesthetically, with its pipes arranged precisely to enhance the appearance of the church, and it tells the world, resoundingly clearly, that this is a place of worship that sets great store by its music. It was built by the long-established J.W. Walker company, then of Ruislip but now operating from Devizes, to the specific design of the parish organist of the day, Ernest Fry, who as we have noted was universally known as Bill. In truth it bore considerable similarities to its larger sister in Liverpool's Roman Catholic Cathedral, but differed in having a mechanical key action; all very exciting, and it looked marvellous, but the keying and wind system were not an unqualified success and in 2015 the organ underwent a considerable redesign and overhaul at the hands of Nicholson and Co. of Worcestershire, at a cost of some £300,000. The company relished the work, and was happy that it was completed well before the 2018 anniversary: 'Now the organ's full potential can at last be achieved, while remaining true to the spirit of its time,' they say.

A day of perfect weather greeted the consecration on July 1, 1967; this was just as well, as the processions and ceremonial began outside, with the sprinkling of the walls. Inside, at the foundation stone, Robert Potter presented the keys to Father Luetchford, a ceremony followed by the singing of *Veni, Creator Spiritus*, the hallowing of the font and the consecration of the altars – the high altar being of polished Portland stone that might be

Robert Potter's striking ceiling emphasises the uncompromising originality of almost every aspect of today's church building

mistaken for marble – by the Bishops of Bristol and Malmesbury. The latter was the Right Revd. Leofric Bishop; Bishop Bishop, indeed, and as predictive names were quite a talking point in the Sixties, thanks not least to the (fairly major) character Major Major in the cult novel *Catch 22*, he found himself smiling bravely through any number of feeble jokes in his eleven years at Malmesbury. As for the 'Leofric', not many people are named after Lady Godiva's other half; but rather like A.A. Milne's James James Morrison Morrison Weatherby George Dupree, the bishop was commonly known as Jim.

After the altars were consecrated the diocesan chancellor then read the sentence of consecration, and on signing it Bishop Oliver Tomkins pronounced the consecration. There then followed mass, the sermon by the Right Revd. Mervyn Stockwood, which is reproduced at the back of this book, and choral music which not only highlighted the tone and power of the new organ but the splendour of the choir's new livery. 'I'm happy to record the pleasant sense of admiration and relief I felt on seeing it,' one anxious member of the congregation reported. 'I confess I had earlier anxieties about the success of the change.'

As well as Robert Potter, several men and women involved in the rebuilding were present, not least John Piper, as were a large number of priests past and present, representatives of other religions, the constituency M.P. and, once again, Cyril Clarke. All of this might have been expected, give or take the odd surprise visitor, but rather more touchingly, solemn evensong the following Sunday was attended by the foreman and several men who had helped build the church, employees of the contractors Cowlin. After the service they, their families and friends gathered in what was temporarily once again the parish hall for 'a splendid party with an excellent buffet supper', prepared by Mothers' Union members and served up by Guides and Brownies. 'It was a most happy occasion by which to express our gratitude to them for our two years of friendship,' the church magazine's report on the event concludes warmly.

The *Bristol Evening Post* devoted three stories to the consecration over four days – a photograph of the tower and spire on June 30, a picture page on the big day and a diary column two days later, on July 3. The spire story was short and packed with facts and statistics of the kind newspapers (and indeed many readers) love – a £4,000 aluminium-clad structure in laminated Douglas fir, seventy-seven feet high and sitting atop a sixty-three foot tower. The spire was the last feature of the building to be put in place, first the tapering timber base and then the aluminium sleeve lowered on top of it; already it had become part of local folklore, raised into position by a massive crane which was said to be the loftiest in Europe at the time. Some people could never believe that such a structure could have been placed other than by a hovering helicopter but prosaic as it seems, a crane it was; not that it did not cause considerable stir and disruption on the day, with a crowd of some eight hundred milling around to watch the show.

The main *Evening Post* story, on the day of the consecration, was surrounded by five photographs, not one of which conveyed any impression of the church, inside or out. The main one showed four Girl Guides smiling prettily through the war memorial arch and apparently 'admiring the crucifix' at its apex. Others showed Bishop Tomkins and clergy, a general processional scene, Cyril Clarke with his wife and Father Luetchford leading the Lord Mayor – the formidable Alderman and Revd. Frederick C. Vyvyan-Jones – into church. Much of the accompanying article seemed equally peripheral to the point, though there were again some statistics to be mulled over. The cost of the building, the paper had been told, was around £128,000, with the windows another £12,300 and the furnishings excluding the organ a further £6,000. War damage contributions were £106,300 plus £10,728 for the windows. The congregation for the service was estimated at some five hundred.

Two days later, on July 3, came the *Evening Post*'s most thoughtful coverage, in the Blackboy's Diary gossip column. Unusually, it was written at that time by Richard Taylor, one of the newspaper's directors and a mature commentator well versed in the ways of the city. The main thrust of his piece was inspired by Mervyn Stockwood's sermon, but the writer took time to reflect: 'Many more than those who attended the consecration of the restored

The pine inner structure of the new church spire begins its long ascent to the top of the tower. The crane that did the job, when extended, was the loftiest in Europe

Not quite as the original architect George Street envisaged it, but the spire now makes a significant impact on the Pembroke Road skyline

church of All Saints, Clifton on Saturday will, I hope, take an opportunity to visit it. The new building forms a striking contrast to its predecessor, giving a fine impression of light and space while capturing the reverent atmosphere which is essential to a place of worship. On entering, one is immediately struck by the long vertical panels of crimson stained glass (sic) which flank the altar. I am not quite so happy about some of the other glass, though this is a personal opinion which others might not share.'

Mr. Taylor then adds, seemingly with feeling: 'The long and complicated ritual of Saturday's service must have made it something of an ordeal for those taking part.' But he establishes his wakefulness throughout the proceedings when he adds: 'I may not be alone when I admit my own ignorance when I listened to the Bishop of Bristol say the words: "Prevent us, O Lord, in all our doings with thy most gracious favour..." Prevent? Yes indeed. There is an archaic definition of the word which means to anticipate a wish by satisfying it.' A pleasant, thoughtful note on which to end the paper's coverage of the consecration.

Of course, a year later, in the summer of 1968, there was another milestone to be marked – the centenary of the original church. After all the high emotion of 1967 'It is not easy to determine what we are to celebrate,' a contributor to the June '68 parish magazine mused, before warming to his task and pondering on all the hopes, prayers and offerings that found their fulfilment in that consecration ceremony of June 8, 1868. Not only that, but 'One hundred years have passed, during which it has been our privilege and joy not only to set a high standard of worship but also to serve the church in the diocese and beyond. It is natural and right that we should rejoice in all that has been accomplished, but we can only do so provided that we look beyond and outside the walls of this church.

'It of course must be the power house, hence the importance of using it to the full for private devotion, which in the presence of the holy sacrament is creative of an atmosphere which is infectious. The new church already has such an atmosphere, and many visitors have told how they feel compelled to repeat the visit over and over again... The centenary celebrations which coincide with the first dedication festival of the new church mark the beginning of a new chapter.' This outward-looking message is as relevant now as it was fifty years ago – and happily, it is still being hearteningly heeded by today's worshippers.

Leading up to the centenary, on May 19, the BBC televised solemn mass from All Saints, and the striking interior of the new church became known to thousands of people from beyond the diocese for the first time. The programme's producer was Kenneth Savidge, who specialised in religious broadcasting from Bristol and counted among his most high-profile work *Songs of Praise* and John Betjeman's *ABC of Churches*, made at a time when the poet laureate was revelling in reviving his West Country connections. The All Saints parish magazine was certainly appreciative of Mr. Savidge's approach: 'All who took part were hardly conscious of the presence and movement of the television team, which is a great tribute to the reverence and devotion with which they do their intricate jobs.'

The musical highlight of the centenary celebrations was a concert on July 4 with the choir, organ and a young brass ensemble to the fore. The blind French organist and composer Jean Langlais's *Missa Salve Regina* was at the heart of the programme, with the congregation taking an active part in both the rehearsal and the final presentation. It was a time when the organist and choirmaster Ernest Fry was taking a keen interest in modern church music from France, not least the Taizé community, and through a contact at Prinknash Abbey in Gloucestershire he had persuaded the charismatic Dom Laurence Bevenot to write a descant mass especially for the All Saints centenary. Bevenot had spent many not particularly happy years teaching at Ampleforth, but in the end his superiors had taken pity on him and sent him out preaching, and by the time Ernest Fry had made contact with him he had moved down to Cardiff as an assistant priest. The way Bevenot went about it, this at last left plenty of time for music.

Like Langlais, Bevenot was strongly influenced by modal music and plainsong, and when his descant mass was used at high mass on September 15, 1968 it was again not surprisingly felt wise to precede the service with a rehearsal for all. Those who remember these occasions recall them as unusual but singularly rewarding times, a glimpse of life on the other side of the conductor's baton. The July 4 concert continued with plainsong and two motets by a far earlier French composer, Francois Couperin, before concluding with the choir and brass revelling in *Christus Vincit* by the Belgian Flor Peeters on his sixty-fifth birthday.

Almost immediately after the centenary Father Luetchford, a traditionalist who by chance had found himself at the heart of the church's most progressive and radical chapter in its history, stepped down to make way for Father John Norton, who moved south from a parish in Sunderland but had previously been an assistant at St. Mary Redcliffe and had often visited All Saints in its Little Church days. Father Luetchford continued to live in the Bristol area and for some years was chaplain to the Sisters of Charity at Knowle, a group always close to All Saints' heart and a friend indeed in the dark days of December 1940. Looking back over his twenty-two years, he mused: 'It seems only yesterday that I came to

Father Albert Luetchford delivers up the new building in Christopher Webb's somewhat whimsical memorial window in the St. Richard chapel

you as a stranger. They have been hard and exacting years, but by God's help we have together managed to survive without any major disaster!' He said one of his greatest joys had been that during his ministry, no fewer than ten young men from the choir school and parish had been ordained. That, indeed, is quite a record.

Also in Father Luetchford's time came the combination of All Saints and St. Mary, Tyndall's Park into a parish in 1962, a pairing that remained until 1976, when the latter was joined with St. Saviour, Redland. This joint parish then bought the redundant Highbury Chapel, which was restored and rededicated to St. Saviour and St. Mary, Cotham to replace both buildings. At one time the BBC used the Tyndall's Park church as a scenery store but it is now the evangelical Woodlands Christian Centre, with supported housing on an upper floor.

On his last Sunday, July 28, 1968, Father Luetchford preached at both St. Mary's and All Saints, where the morning service congregation numbered more than three hundred. Later in the day the Mothers' Union was busy again in the parish hall, with a buffet supper after evensong to bid the vicar farewell. Because he was such a strong traditionalist, he was some-

How to bridge the void between the Edwardian narthex on the left and the Victorian tower base on the right? The architect Potter had a spectacular answer to that

times the butt of gentle humour for his non-progressive ways. He was never at ease with the concept of preparing the sacrament facing the congregation, rather than with his back to it, and some joked that this was because he preferred not to be facing John Piper's baptistry windows. There was also the story, apocryphal or not, that he had said there would be women choristers at All Saints over his dead body; and so it came to pass many years later, when the church's by now mixed choir sang at his funeral.

Shortly afterwards, with the coming of Father Norton came the departure of Father Geoffrey Sunderland, who had proved a popular assistant priest during two spells at All Saints. He left to become Vicar of Plymstock in Devon, and was there until his retirement eighteen years later. From 1981 until '89 he further served as a prebendary of Exeter Cathedral, by which time his days of buzzing around Clifton on his old bike must have seemed a distant memory. Father Sunderland lived on until 2013, and was ninety-one when he died.

Another departure at much this time, and another sad one, was the death of Father Cyril Tomkinson on June 5, 1968 – three days before the official centenary. In truth he had been gravely ill for some time, so there would never have been any question of his joining in the celebrations, but he was in the thoughts of many as the priest who just a year after his arrival was plunged into the horror of December 2, 1940. The notice of his death in the July, 1968 church magazine was brief but sincere: 'He is remembered with affection, for it was he who secured the continuance of church life and worship at a time when many people despaired of the future.' He was, in truth, not the only one who saw potential in that somewhat unpromising parish hall; but he was there at the forefront of keeping the dream alive.

The Little Church, once more the parish hall, saw another decade or more's useful service until, with the church and atrium coming increasingly into play as a gathering point for social events, it was felt to be dispensable and was sold in the early 1980s. Not that its charms were always appreciated by those who used it. On one occasion it had been hired for an exam for a group of masseurs, complete with skeleton, and somehow or other they found themselves locked in. Perhaps somewhat over-dramatically, they called the fire brigade, and the first one-time churchwarden Andrew Morgan heard about it was when a neighbour told him: 'There's been a terrible fire at All Saints! I saw a skeleton carried out!'

After Father Norton's departure in 1981 there was the brief incumbency of the Revd. Jeremy Younger before Father Peter Cobb's twenty-year ministry began in 1984. He retired in 2004 to make way for Richard Hoyal, and there was a large congregation for his funeral requiem at All Saints in June, 2010. He had a colourful assistant priest from 1987 into the following year in Diarmaid MacCulloch, who tutored at Wesley College in Bristol and taught church history at Bristol University while interrupting this work to study for the priesthood. He became a deacon in 1987, immediately taking up his non-stipendiary post at All Saints, but declined full ordination in response to a motion put before the General Synod in 1987 regarding the sexuality of clergy. Now an academic specialising in the heritage of Christianity, he has been Professor of the History of the Church at Oxford since 1997 as well as a successful writer and creator of several television documentaries. The six-part series *A History of Christianity* has been seen twice on BBC4 and also on BBC2, while among other ventures, in 2013 he presented a documentary on Thomas Cromwell's place in English ecclesiastical and political history.

An over-riding issue in the Church of England in the final years of the last century was the question of women in the priesthood, with a ground-swell in favour and traditional Anglo-Catholic and Evangelical churches voicing strong reservations. Food for thought for them in this diocese was the fact that Bishop Barry Rogerson was a leading supporter of the move, and on March 12, 1994 he ordained the first thirty-two women priests in the Church of England.

Left and opposite: natural abundance in the church garden acts as a memorable foil to the building's striking symmetry

Aware of the controversy the move would cause, the House of Bishops provided for churches which on grounds of theological conviction were 'unable to receive the ministry of women bishops or priests' to be given the opportunity to opt out by resolving A, that they would not be willing to have a woman licensed in the parish; B, to officiate in this parish; and C, that they would request that instead of the diocesan bishop, a provincial episcopal visitor or 'flying bishop' would have oversight over their church. Shortly after the arrival of Father Richard Hoyal in 2004 the P.C.C. voted on this issue and passed all three of the resolutions, with the Bishop of Ebbsfleet becoming the church's episcopal visitor.

A condition of the arrangement was that the P.C.C. should have a further say whenever the parish went into vacancy, so after Father Hoyal's departure in 2014 the issue arose again. It was not a happy time in the All Saints story, with strongly-held feelings on both sides of the debate, but after an uneasy parish meeting the P.C.C. voted once again – and this time reversed its earlier decision and endorsed women in the priesthood. A number of worshippers left – not all of them older members of the congregation – seeking to uphold their tradition at other Anglican churches or along Pembroke Road at Clifton Cathedral. Some

have returned to All Saints since then, and of course newcomers have come along. As for those who have stayed, a number confess that they have done so while still being unhappy with the change. And of course, there are are many strongly convinced that the move to ordain women priests from bishops downwards is the just, right and proper one.

It must be said that as the years went by before its decision was reversed, All Saints was drawing some disobliging comments in quite high-profile places. Writing in *The Guardian* in 2010, as the Church of England was nearing its approval of women as bishops, the Revd. Clare Herbert recalled: 'I became a deaconess when I was in my mid-twenties and worked as a parish worker and university chaplain in Bristol. The first time I preached at All Saints Church in Clifton, they genuinely thought that the marble (sic) on top of the altar might crack when I spoke, and when it came to taking communion from a woman – and I was only administering the chalice – a lot of people refused.' At much the same time a correspondent on a well-read website that specialises in visiting churches anonymously wrote glowingly about his All Saints experience – but stressed that he would not consider joining the church because of its stance on women priests.

In January, 1995 All Saints attracted national attention when it emerged that Mervyn Stockwood had asked for his funeral to be there. Some in the congregation were not surprised; after all, it had been his childhood church after his family had moved to Bristol from Wales when he was very young, and his deep affection for the original building and its people had shone through very clearly when he preached the sermon at the consecration in 1967. On the other hand, he so loved a show that others were surprised that he had not plumped for a more high-profile venue in London; after all, twenty-one years as Bishop of Southwark had been no passing blip in his life.

Llamas substitute for camels at an Epiphany procession in early 2018. The reverent way in which this one is seen listening to the sermon suggests that the switch was a good choice

It is alleged that when asked about his funeral wishes, his response had been 'No fuss, dear, no fuss', Tim Stanley recalls, but in the event it was a huge event. His coffin had been taken to the church the previous evening and carefully positioned before the altar to ensure that his head was within the sanctuary, on the altar side of the communion rail. The high and exotic Anglo-Catholic mass the next day started with a procession of several bishops – including the then Archbishop of Canterbury – and throughout the service they stood in a semi-circle behind the altar, creating a backdrop reminiscent of the saintly reredos and east window of George Street's original church.

One of Jessica Smith's abiding memories of being churchwarden from 1994 to '98 is of 'wanding in' those bishops with her fellow warden Norman Drewett. Her recollection, and she should know, is that there were eight, including the Archbishop – but such was the impression they made that some members of the congregation that day will still shake their heads in wonderment and swear that 'ooh, there were dozens of 'em'. Later Mrs. Smith, widow of the long-serving organist Ken, trained to be a Reader, and was licensed in 2005, the first woman to hold that role in this church.

After Mervyn Stockwood's funeral, several parishioners gathered in the Alma Tavern to share their memories of one of the most colourful and controversial character in All Saints' – and arguably the entire Church of England's – history. One year during an interregnum he came from his home in Bath for Holy Week and Easter to support the two young curates who were holding the fort, Fathers Robert Pyne and George Bennett – and on Easter Day, to the delight of all, he interrupted the service to tell them: 'There are birds of paradise in my garden, and they have laid these eggs for you because you have worked so hard.' He then handed each of them a gaily-wrapped package containing eggs suspiciously shaped like Gordon's Gin and Johnnie Walker Whisky bottles. At the same service he preached a memorable sermon with so many funny stories that everyone laughed throughout.

He told about an Easter he had spent in the Holy Land, when his hosts entertained him with an extravagant banquet in which the ultimate delicacies were sheep's eyes. He was revolted when he was ceremoniously presented with one, but not wishing to upset his hosts he said: 'You have already been so very kind and generous to me that I wish to pass this great honour on to my curate!' Another member of the congregation after the funeral recalled that she had been confirmed by Mervyn Stockwood as an adult, and had been impressed by the fact that his cassock had seemed to be of finest shot silk; impressed, but somehow not surprised.

It was in the March of 2004 that the church enjoyed the stimulus of a new vicar in fifty-six-year-old Canon Richard Hoyal, who for the past fourteen years had been vicar of St. Margaret's Church, Ilkely in Yorkshire. To his delighted amusement, he was replaced there in the August by no less than Dr. David Hope, who wished to exchange the trappings of high office as Archbishop of York for a more simple parish life. In a number of ways Father Hoyal was a High Church traditionalist and was and still is heartily admired as such by many, but his moves to build up the congregation were strictly early twenty-first century, with an emphasis on encouraging young families.

For instance, in 2006 he brought new life to the annual service at the war memorial outside the former St. John's Church at the junction of Apsley Road and Whiteladies Road to mark Remembrance Day. It is from that church's territory, of course, that the original All Saints sprang up, and it was when the building was made redundant in the 1980s that the present parish of All Saints with St. John Clifton was formed. That first year, Father Hoyal was joined by a handful of parishioners and a few passers-by in a short act of remembrance. Now attendances run into their hundreds, with pupils and teachers from some seven schools and other organisations taking part. It is very much an event to remind young people of the consequences of war, rather than for the older generation.

Retired Lieutenant Colonel Steen Clarke, a former pupil of St. John's Church of England Primary School, became involved with the committee and organised the restoration and cleaning of the Grade II Listed memorial. He also pointed out to the school that most of the men named on the memorial were once pupils there and more than forty of its children attended a service of rededication to mark the restoration in 2016. The colonel also under-took extensive research into the fate of twenty-seven former pupils named on the memorial who died fighting in Belgium, France and particularly at the Battle of the Somme in 1916,

It is what a parish church does in its community that is important – but what a base from which to go out into the world!

while later he turned his attention to another ten who lost their lives in Greece, Italy, Egypt, Iraq and Syria.

In the centenary year of that dreadful waste of life on the Somme, and on the tenth anniversary of Richard Hoyal's revival of the ceremony, the then Bishop of Bristol, Mike Hill, led proceedings assisted by Father Charles Sutton, who replaced Father Richard in 2015, and other clergy from Churches Together in Clifton, Cotham and Redland. A bugler, piper and brass players from Redland High Junior School who accompanied the hymn 'I Vow to Thee, my Country' and the National Anthem ensured that this was a ceremony performed with all due reverence and gravity.

In 2008 John Davenport replaced Graham Davies as the church's organist, choirmaster and director of music, having retired from teaching and directing in schools that included Clifton College. All Saints Arts had recently been put into place to expand, organise and promote the church's already established programme of wider artistic and musical events and Mr. Davenport, with his close contacts with a number of choirs, ensembles and orchestras in the West Country, has been ideally placed to make this flourish – not least in his contribution to the programme to mark the church's 150th anniversary.

As for the church choir, which became adult-only with women singing soprano and alto after the choir school closed, there are around twenty members and there might be some fifteen present on an average Sunday. Mr. Davenport is enthusiastic about the siting of the choir stalls, facing and towards the rear of the congregation. 'They're brilliant,' he says. 'They give the choir a real presence as far as the congregation is concerned, and as an organist I can direct the singers very easily. In fact the entire church layout is inspirational for music. The acoustic is very fine for a chamber choir and even a group of up to seventy or eighty sounds good.' For much of the year, he says, the choir is enhanced by some 'super, enthusiastic' students from Bristol University; sadly, of course, they tend to be elsewhere at Easter, Christmas and some of the other major festivals.

On a typical Sunday the choir leads the congregation in one of six mass settings, while on high days and major holy days they turn to a more demanding repertoire with masses by masters including Byrd, Palestrina, Mozart, Haydn and Schubert. A motet while mass is being taken by the congregation is another welcome and prized aspect of regular worship. As noted, like some other aspects of the church, the organ was beginning to show its age by the early years of this millennium, and equally, like much else at the 1967 All Saints, its design was experimental in several aspects, not least its tracker action. Mr. Davenport, an organist well known throughout Bristol and beyond for his skill, was deeply involved in its £300,000 restoration in 2015. And was it worth it? 'Worth it? It's fantastic!'

Between Richard Hoyal's retirement and the arrival of Charles Sutton in 2015 there was the brief transitional incumbency of Kim Taplin, the former chaplain at Clifton College who was shortly to take up a chaplaincy post back in education at Malvern St. James School in Worcestershire. For Father Charles it was no great change of scene since he had been a self-supporting assistant priest at All Saints since 2012, most of his working life being spent as an organisational psychologist in industry. Very soon after his appointment as vicar he was asked by the diocese to take on the additional role of bishops' adviser for self-supporting ministry, and he relishes this additional brief. 'I've become increasingly intrigued by how self-supporting ministers fit into the life of the church, especially as we are rapidly becoming such a huge part of how it works,' he says. 'After all, in the Diocese of Bristol, self-supporting ministers and ordained licensed ministers make up around half our clergy.'

Being steeped in helping to make things tick, either at All Saints or in large multinational companies, Father Charles is hugely appreciative of all who contribute to the life of the church, both professional and voluntary. And he cannot disguise his satisfaction that when Richard Hoyal's departure set in train a second P.C.C. vote on the role of women in the Church of England, the original outcome was reversed.

'Rescinding our decision on ABC was a significant moment in the history of the church, but not necessarily a sea change,' he says. 'This has always been a more accepting, diverse and mission-proactive church, and that has been an important feature. One of the things the resolutions did while they were in place was to create a little pause to think carefully about where we wanted to be. I know people might look at this as a traditional Anglo-Catholic church. It is true that it has always kept its Catholic nature, but it has also maintained its very active, open and welcoming style.'

One tradition certainly being upheld in full is All Saints' commitment to being an outward-looking church intent on helping others, far and near, in a variety of ways. At specific times of year it dedicates its collections at services to an agreed charity, while ensuring that five per cent of its annual income is given to carefully chosen good causes, balanced between local and international Christian charities. A prime example of the latter is the church's support through partnership of the Missio Dei school in Amuru, Northern Uganda.

The siting of the choir stalls to the side and rear of the congregation is widely seen as one of the architect's masterstrokes

Other recently supported charities have included Emmaus Bristol, which works for homeless and socially excluded people, the Julian Trust night shelter, the Salvation Army, Christian Aid and Water Aid. Over and above that, All Saints aims to be a dementia-friendly church, not only in its donations to the Alzheimer's Society but with a Friends' Café and Sunday afternoon worship both designed to be dementia-appropriate. In this anniversary year the church is supporting the work of Off the Record, a mental health social movement for young people aged from eleven to twenty-five in Bristol and South Gloucestershire. The organisation prides itself on the imaginative variety of projects it has on offer, and the unobtrusive free and confidential support that comes with it. 'Much of our outreach is an observable engagement in activities focused on the care of those in need in Bristol and beyond,' says Father Charles. 'However, many of those at All Saints also volunteer and give time and support to a variety of agencies in a way that is often unobserved, yet is very much a part of their respect of creation and how they see their faith living out in their lives. Others support these works through their lives of prayer, meditation and giving.'

On the eve of its 150th anniversary, All Saints put its commitment to its new approach to Resolutions A, B and C into practice by appointing its first woman priest, the Revd. Wendy Bray. She was licensed in the bishop's chapel by the acting Bishop of Bristol, Lee Rayfield,

Christmas 2016 is greeted at All Saints
in memorable style

on February 1, 2018 and formally welcomed to the church on February 11 at the 11 a.m. parish mass, followed by a reception in the atrium. Mother Wendy – as she is now listed on the All Saints website – was formerly a curate at St. Pancras Church in Plymouth.

As noted, some aspects of the structure of the All Saints building are wearing their age better than others and like many 1960s creations, they are demanding and already receiving quite considerable attention. The roof, the ceiling, the lighting; the facts that the wiring is embedded in concrete and that concrete creates a cold environment; a heating system problematic in a number of ways; as already discussed, the deterioration of the iconic John Piper windows, and the search for remedies: as the church enters its second one hundred and fifty years, those who love it have plenty of food for thought.

Then again, when the programme of events for the 150th celebrations was launched in February, 2018 there was much to think about in a far more cheerful light, with the way being led in terms of music on March 8 with the world premiere of *The River of Life*, a

Sign of the times: a boat girl accompanies
the thurifer in the Palm Sunday procession

major new choral work commissioned by the church with words by Julie Nicholson, a
writer, public speaker and Anglican priest and music by John Marsh, director of music at
Bristol's Lord Mayor's Chapel. The cantata was of course inspired by the baptistry window
and performed by more than one hundred and fifty voices drawn from All Saints' choir,
members of other local choirs and singers from Clifton College, Clifton High School, the
Bristol Cathedral Consort and the St. John's Junior School choral speaking group.

The chief anniversary celebration day was chosen to be Sunday, June 17, with the 11a.m.
festival mass led by the Right Revd. Rachel Treweek, the Bishop of Gloucester, who became
the first female diocesan bishop in the Church of England in June 2015. It was, of course,
the Bishop of Gloucester (and then also of Bristol) who performed the 1868 consecration
ceremony. In other significant worship days pilgrims from Holy Faith, Santa Fe were
expected to be at the Feast of the Assumption on August 15 while it was hoped that the
newly elected Bishop of Bristol would be in office to lead parish mass on October 14.

Ash Wednesday, 2018, with Father Charles Sutton and churchwarden Victoria Gordon standing beside a very modern invitation to a very ancient ceremony

Other musical events announced included a performance of Leonard Bernstein's *Chichester Psalms* by the City of Bristol Choir to mark the conductor's hundredth birthday; a concert by the New Bristol Sinfonia and the violinist Julia Hwang, including Wagner's *Siegfried Idyll*, the Bruch *Violin Concerto* and Beethoven's *Symphony No.7*; and two violin recitals by Thomas Bowes as part of the nationwide Bach Pilgrimage. The announcement of a series of five Saturday afternoon organ recitals between April and October was also warmly welcomed. The programme listed a series of art and photographic exhibitions, including paintings and other works by the church's Randall Artists on show in the atrium and an exhibition in October as part of the Bristol West Art Trail. Saturday afternoon lectures were also scheduled, including Professor Frances Spalding examining 'The Life and Work of John Piper'; while Professor Mark Chapman speaking on 'Catholic Renewal Lives On' in September was another that immediately caught the eye when the programme was announced.

At all these events All Saints Church is welcoming strangers as well as friends, believers and non-believers, visitors from all walks of society. So it has always been, and will continue

The Revd. Wendy Bray, appointed in 2018 as All Saints' first female priest

to be as the years roll on, for this will always take pride in being a place of welcome for all people. All people? 'Yes, it really is,' says Father Charles. 'Lots of people come in every day. I talk about our "irregulars", who don't go to services but can almost be guaranteed to be there at other times of the week. Some come in to light a candle. One man comes in and writes poetry, another to play the piano. One woman who runs past comes in every Saturday morning and just sits there. It's part of her programme. Mind you, if I were running I'd sit there a lot longer than she does!

'Then again, recently a couple of chaps came to the vicarage door. They looked quite concerned and said to me: "Do you know the church is open?"

"Oh yes, good."

"No, no, it's *open*. Anyone can go in."

"Yes."

"But there's a *tramp* in there."

"Well, he's probably sheltering because it's raining."

"So that's OK?"

"Yes. That's more than OK. That's absolutely fine.'"

A church for all people, from its community and beyond:
All Saints as seen from high on the neighbouring Clifton Cathedral

With music at the heart of its worship, the church has always set extraordinary store by the high standard of its choir, and within a very few years of its founding it astonished many of its neighbouring parishes by forming its own school for choristers. This lasted, sometimes precariously, until financial pressures finally put an end to it in 1962; but the fact remains that for the best part of a century, All Saints was able to offer daily choral services, as well as full 'cathedral music' on Sundays.

The first school was in Alma Road, and as the moving forces behind it were the precentor and assistant priest the Revd. T.G. Bowles and the organist, George Riseley, it struck them as only fair that they should be the school's first residents. Their sole aim was to find boys with good voices, turn those voices into better ones, and be in a position to provide a choir for morning services each day of the week. The sacristan and his wife helped with running the school and cooking and the way Forster Alleyne tells it in his book, it seems almost as an afterthought that Messrs. Bowles and Riseley found themselves 'procuring, besides, the help of an efficient schoolmaster'. A teacher named Walter Smith arrived from Oxford, bringing with him a number of pupils, and this was the beginning of an institution more recognisable as a school.

Both of the original founders soon moved out, Mr. Riseley to get married, but even Walter Smith's sudden and unexpected death in 1884 was not the blow it might have been a few years earlier. He was succeeded as headmaster by the Revd. C.H. Richards, and according to Forster Alleyne in 1893, 'under him the school has greatly prospered, and it has already turned out many boys who have done well in after life'. 'Later life' might have been a happier phrase.

It was also in 1884 that the school moved to 9, All Saints Road, bought for £2,000 but with almost as much again spent in additional buildings. Since the money was raised only with the help of a £2,300 mortgage, a number of people in the church felt the school was something of a luxury, and mourned the fact that more could not have been paid off through donations. A full-time choir school certainly seems an extraordinary expense for a parish church today, but it is hard to over-estimate its contribution to the musical heritage of All Saints over the years.

In 1992, Father John Morley-Bunker recalled that he was a member of the school in All Saints Road from 1934, when he joined as its youngest pupil. The boys were expected to attend all the Sunday services, though of course they sometimes fell short of this. On Monday mornings, apart from marking the school register, the teachers noted the services each chorister had attended. For the main morning service he recalled that one of the curates, Father Gurney, would say 'come at 9.45 when it's fine and quarter to ten when it's wet'. Father John admitted that the regime was sometimes hard for the younger boys, and 'when the services got a bit boring, I used to gnaw the back of the chairs. You could see some chairs where I had been sitting for a long time afterwards!' In those early days he was a tassel boy, holding on to the banner tassels in processions on All Saints Day, Easter, Christmas and other major festivals. Later and for many years he was a boat boy, the altar boy who carried the incense boat for the thurifer with the censer.

The choir and clergy led by Father Albert Luetchford in the 1950s, when the church's choir school still played a central role in church life

The Second World War, while of course devastating for the church, was also a trying time for the school. 'To begin with when the sirens started we would go up Thorndale Road, into Alma Vale Road and then into the cellar of the church, which we used as an air raid shelter,' Father John recalled. 'In the end we found there were so many raids we were not getting any work done, so the teachers decided they would just close the shutters in the school and carry on.' An ostrich-like approach, some might say, but in this case it worked.

Later the school spilled over into 70 Pembroke Road, the property adjoining the vicarage which was for years an integral part of church life. 'Every floor holds memories for me, some of them going back to the early 1950s,' says Tim Stanley. 'That was when it played host to the Mothers' Union, who met in the lino-floored rooms on the ground floor and then enjoyed tea and cakes served at a trestle table beneath the sweeping staircase. As small children we were looked after in another room by Mrs. Skerrett, who was very affectionate, assisted by Frances Perkins.

'As a pupil at the choir school in the late 1950s and early 1960s, I made daily visits to the basement of Number Seventy, and the canteen ruled by Mrs. Marks. During morning break we could buy biscuits there and marvel as we peered through the hatch to the kitchen to watch Mrs. Marks chopping the six-foot sausage rolls she had made during the morning into individual portions. They were tasty, but even the thought of the cheese and potato splodge she served at the end of each week – no meat on Fridays – still makes me nauseous. The garden at the rear of Number Seventy was stocked with cabbages, sprouts, carrots and other staples of school dinners – so different from the colourful herbaceous borders that flourished there latterly.'

Mr. Stanley recalls the school's art room on the first floor, where Miss Gulliver's deep voice and apparently nicotine-stained hair belied a kindly nature: 'I found art – painting with water-colours – an enjoyable and relaxing pursuit. Miss Gulliver taught us to draw outlines "in Van Dyke brown, very pale", before she approved our work and let us splash on the colour.

'For a year or two my classroom was relocated from the main school to Number Seventy's airy first-floor room with its bay window, where Miss Alsop tried to drum Latin into our young heads. But the top floor was the most intriguing; it housed the school laboratory, full of benches with sinks and gas taps, Bunsen burners and tripods, pink rubber tubing and strange glass vessels.

'By the time we were old enough to study chemistry and physics the French-Canadian science master Mr. Bertham had left. He was replaced by a man we regarded as the archetypal mad scientist. With hair awry, dishevelled clothes and thick glasses perched on the end of his nose, Mr. Heslop was more entertainer than educator. His experiments frequently went awry as carelessly-mixed chemicals produced foam solutions deadlier than any weapons of mass destruction Saddam Hussain might have been accused of harbouring.

'A timber partition wall with clear glass at the top separated the lab. from a passage linking the top floor of Number Seventy to 68 Pembroke Road, the Vicarage. On that top floor was a flat occupied by two young curates, Father Owen and Father Sanderson. Father Owen was precentor responsible for the choral services and a lot of fun; his impressions of elderly ladies in the congregation were legendary. As for Father Sanderson, I remember him walking through an empty church whistling 'Get Me To The Church On Time' from *My Fair Lady*. Out of Mr. Heslop's line of vision, these two would amuse us by waving handkerchiefs above their heads so they were just visible through the partition glass. One day, as smoke from yet another wayward experiment filled the lab and filtered into their flat, they burst in with their handkerchiefs clamped to their noses to assure us that the fire brigade was on its way!'

A near-contemporary of Tim Stanley at the school and another lifelong member of the church, including three spells as churchwarden, is Andrew Morgan. He recalls choir practices every day, sometimes taking precedence over lessons, and evensong in the Little Church three or four times a week, as well as at festivals. He also looks back on those times when the choir sang in the open, in the ruins of the bombed church.

He remembers how in many ways boys would be boys, tearing off on their bikes to Clifton Down railway station to stand precariously on their saddles and reach up to turn off the gas lamps that survived there anachronistically into the Swinging Sixties. But he also remembers how sometimes boys could seem little lower than angels under Bill Fry's meticulous direction. 'What a marvellous musical tradition that man gave us,' he recalls. 'I remember how we surprised visitors from Wales, over for the day to visit the zoo, by the wonderful music they heard coming from an ordinary looking house in All Saints Road.'

Oddly, the old boy of the school who made the greatest mark in music did so in a very different tradition from choral singing. Trevor Stanford was a pupil in the years immediately before the Second World War, and though his first career choice was as a merchant seaman, it was as the pianist Russ Conway that he won fame, with seven Top Ten hits between 1959 and 1961, including two Number Ones in 1959 with 'Side Saddle', which stayed in the charts for thirty weeks, and 'Roulette', a big seller for nineteen weeks. He was also constantly on television at a time when variety shows were staple fare, and his many 'Party Pops' albums sold prodigiously.

Tim Stanley, who was at the school at the height of Trevor's fame, says his progress was monitored carefully by the boys and staff. Apparently Bill Fry, no mean keyboard player himself, of course, told the lads that while Russ Conway's right hand played the tune his left hand, which had some fingers missing, did little more than hammer out the bass beat. Maybe it was that that gave him such a distinctive sound. It certainly did not do his career any harm.

But was Trevor Stanford in the All Saints choir? From this distance it is hard to know, and the man himself died of cancer in 2000 at the age of seventy-five. 'One year I won the Singing Cup, and among the engraved names of earlier winners was Trevor's,' says Mr. Stanley. 'However, that was a school cup, rather than exclusively for the choristers, so I don't know whether or not he was in the choir.'

He certainly would have been if Bill Fry had been around in his day.

'Bill' Fry, an inspirational choirmaster

Tim Stanley remembers a hard taskmaster and an outstanding servant to All Saints

It was a few years after Edward Fry – always known as Bill – arrived at All Saints in the early 1950s as a young man with a beard that I joined the choir school in All Saints Road. At that time three of us were probationers wearing cassocks without surplices until our singing had reached an acceptable standard. There was little formal training but during choir practices he would shout to the older boys next to us 'Point to the babies! Point to the babies!' – as if, by following our neighbour's finger on the score, we would acquire the skill of singing the right notes.

Somehow it worked and, under Bill Fry's direction in our cramped Little Church in Alma Vale Road we sang the great masses – Stanford, Gibbons and Kirby all come to mind – as well as works by Byrd and Palestrina and Allegri's *Miserere*. We sang Gregorian chant at evensong most nights, including weekends and during school holidays, and the service was preceded by a choir practice. Even today as I round the corner into All Saints Road I have

The choir gathered around the organ behind the altar in the Little Church – an odd arrangement, but one that served its purpose

a slight dread that I will hear psalms drifting from the bay window of Number 9, confirming that I am late and about to incur the wrath of Mr. Fry.

He was not slow to make his feelings felt – loudly and persistently. We were frequently admonished in triplicate with the emphasis on the verb third time around. 'I hate you! I hate you! I hate you!' Maybe because of this, standards were high – very high. We were told our choir, men and boys, was the best church choir in the South West of England. It might have been true. Certainly we were one of the first in the country to tackle the new and highly complex Benjamin Britten Mass and make a success of it.

Even a single wrong note was not tolerated, and in practice the boy responsible could expect to be mocked loudly in no uncertain terms: 'Donkey! Donkey! Donkey!' During a service, when Bill's organ console was between the choir stalls behind the high altar, the error was simply met with a protruding tongue and repeated looks of extreme distaste being shot at the boy for the rest of the service. The clergy were not immune to similar treatment. Singing the *Nunc Dimittis* during evensong, Father Brightman, a venerable priest who as the precentor was responsible for choral services, would intone 'And to be the glory of thy people Israel', which he pronounced Is-ry-el. He, too, would get 'the look'.

Sometimes there were treats, like the Christmas visit to a film or a show – which is how I came to see one of the last performances by George Formby at Bristol Hippodrome. In summer there was the annual choir outing to Weymouth, when Bill boarded the coach equipped with mops, buckets, sponges and disinfectant in case someone was travel sick. In fact he took care of his choristers in several ways. At the school's annual cross-country run through Blaise Woods he would be at the start line on the university playing fields in Coombe Lane handing out giant glucose tablets in the hope that his boys would outrun their fellow pupils.

Evensong sometimes had its lighter moments, especially on verse 20 of psalm 136, when we giggled as we chanted: 'And Og the king of Basan...' OG was the first part of the registration number of Bill's ancient Austin 7, so that was what we called it. It was so old that he kept a large enamel jug of water in the back in case the radiator boiled over and the story went that one day, as he was driving an aunt around Piccadilly Circus, her feet went through the floorboards. He would drive economically, saving petrol when he could. Before our Sunday morning choir practice at school he would play the organ during a service at St. Monica Home, and then dash across the Downs to get to us by 10.30. As he sped down

Pembroke Road he would push the car's gears into neutral, turn off the engine, take the corner wide as he swept into All Saints Road and then freewheel until he came to a silent stop outside Number 9.

In many ways the ceaseless demands on us as choristers and Bill Fry's rigid discipline ruled our young lives. A few days before his funeral, after he had died at the age of ninety-five, there was a discussion about education on the radio in which someone said that the teachers for whom we have the greatest regard are the ones who were the strictest disciplinarians. In my case at least, he was right. Mr. Fry sometimes put the fear of God into us – or so we thought then. In later years I realise that he was actually instilling in some of us a lifelong love of church and organ music.

As an organist, he excelled. The voluntaries he played at the end of high mass were often thrilling, and Karg-Elert's uplifting *March Triomphale*, played at the end of his funeral, was a regular favourite. His accompaniment to our Gregorian chant at evensong was timeless and beautiful, and his skilful 'filling in' with what he dubbed 'Original Fry' during the ceremonial was superb. He wrote the music for a mass which is still sung at All Saints periodically – and for many years his memorial was the Walker organ, which he helped to design right down to the words inscribed on the case – *Te Deum Laudamus*. I can hear him saying those words now – with the emphasis, of course, on the last one.

'Let us be careful lest we are lulled to sleep'

_____

Bishop Mervyn Stockwood's sermon at the consecration of the present church, July 1, 1967

Isaiah 51, verse 1: 'Look at the rock whence you were hewn, the quarry from which you were dug. Look at your father Abraham.' **Isaiah 51, verse 1**: 'Bestir yourself, bestir yourself, O Sion, robe yourself with strength.'

These two verses can be summed up in a single sentence: 'Look back in order that you may look forward.'

The Jews were in exile. Having suffered much they doubted their ability to return to Jerusalem to take up the threads again. Their numbers were small. So the Lord speaks to them: 'Your present position may be unpromising, but look back on the much more unpromising conditions of years ago. Today you may be a mere handful, but at least you are a handful. Then it was only one man, Abraham. And such was the faith of this one man that he triumphed. So, then, look at the rock whence you were hewn, the quarry from which you were dug. Look at your father, Abraham. Bestir yourself, and robe yourself with strength.

In 1917 a small boy was standing in the tower porch waiting for morning prayer to finish so that he could take his seat for high mass. He was in fact a very small boy, only four years old, and he had forgotten to remove his cap. So the sacristan, Mr. Edwards, advanced towards him and removed it: 'Caps are not allowed'. Fifty years have passed and that small boy, now half a century older, is back at All Saints, and sometimes he does wear a hat in church because now he's allowed to! Yes, there must be many here this morning who, like myself, find this a deeply moving occasion.

All Saints has played such a big part in our lives. There are so many memories, so many precious moments. Here I came to catechism under Father Gent and Father Hitchcock; here I was confirmed by Bishop Nickson; here I made my first confession and attended my first retreat. And what of those other occasions – the midnight mass at Christmas, with Canon Gillson with majestic dignity blessing the crib. The Palm Sunday ceremonies with the magnificent procession. The orchestra at high mass during the octave when the choir sang Schubert. And those nuances of light and sound which can be known only to those who experienced them – the smell of incense on entering the narthex, the creaking of the

The Right Revd. Mervyn Stockwood, former Bishop of Southwark and
a life-long friend of All Saints.
© Bath In Time www.bathintime.co.uk

chairs on the tiles as the worshipper took his seat, the curtain drawn in the Lady chapel with a narrow gap through which could be seen the flickering sanctuary lamp in front of the sacrament, the scent from the lilies around the font on Easter morning.

But I must not allow these nostalgic reminiscences to obtrude, for to those who did not know the old All Saints they must seem tedious. Suffice it to say, the church had an extraordinary hold on us. It evoked a strange love and a deep loyalty as it pointed us in worship to the reality of God and the mysteries of the Catholic faith. Then came 1940. I was in Bristol on the night of the disaster. It so happened that on the following evening Father Tomkinson had asked me to supper. I shall never forget the two of us standing in the smouldering ruin, the smell of burnt wood, the water, the devastation. It seemed impossible that such a fate could have overtaken our beloved All Saints. But as I look back I see there was a lesson to be learnt. Perhaps we had become too dependent upon a building. Perhaps we had become too fond. In any case, now was the test of our faith and to the Risen Christ we had to turn, ready to travel light with little in our rucksacks but the basic truths that we had learnt here in happier days. That was a long time ago, twenty-seven years. Now, to the site of those early triumphs – and of the subsequent devastation – we are called back...

'Bestir yourself, O Sion, robe yourself with strength.' Let me be severely practical. Just because this church had such a reputation and counted for so much, we may have doubts about its future. Can All Saints ever be the same again? The answer is no, if by 'the same again' we mean a reproduction of what used to be. In those days people came in their hundreds to All Saints because it was one of the few churches that taught the full Catholic faith. Now, thank God, that is no longer true. The fact is, All Saints did the pioneering job so well that it is no longer required for that purpose. Today it has other purposes to serve. This is a parish church, and its primary purpose is to be the headquarters of the local Christian community. Here the members of that community are to be nurtured in the faith and, through the ministry of word and sacrament, learn to work and witness as Christians.

Here the Christian community must be inspired and taught to concern itself with the needs of the people who live in the streets of the parish, whether or not they come to church. Remember, an acid test of churchmanship is to find out how much a church counts in the neighbourhood. It is not what happens inside a church building, but what we do when we leave the church building that spells out the quality of our obedience. Of course, this implies faithfulness in Catholic discipline – but it requires something more, a readiness to serve the people among whom we live. In the old days the whole of Bristol, and beyond, was our catchment area, if not our parish. Today the boundaries are more limited, but not less important.

The climate is unfavourable, and to win this parish to Christ will demand everything we have to give. And we are more likely to do this if we remember two things. First, there must be no looking back. It is right that today we should relive the past, but as soon as this festival is over that chapter in our book must be closed. Those of us who helped to write it will occasionally turn its pages in the privacy of our hearts, but not in public. Whether we are by the waters of Babylon or in Clifton, there must be no sitting down to weep as we recall the memories of a Sion that is no more. Nothing will depress the rising generation more, nothing will do more damage to an advancing cause than to mourn the glories of the days that have vanished. If we think we once lived in a golden age, let us keep that opinion to ourselves and concentrate our efforts on the present.

The second point follows from the first. It is not only from the thoughts of the past that we must free ourselves, but also from the methods. What produced results fifty years ago might not produce results today. And if our antiphon is 'But this is what we used to do – As It Was In The Beginning etc.' – we might succeed in closing our ears to the Spirit. Those of us who are in touch with the Roman Catholic Church know that a revolution is going on, in method and approach, that must be painful to many of its members. But Rome has been pitchforked out of the past into the present, not least by its stern experiences in countries under communist regimes. To survive it has had to adapt.In this country religion is still tolerated and we have an Established Church. Let us be careful lest we are lulled to sleep.

If we are to survive we too must adapt ourselves to the needs of this generation. 'Bestir yourself, bestir yourself, O Sion, and robe yourself with strength' is a command that must not be disobeyed. God summons the new All Saints to tasks different from and probably more difficult than the tasks of older days. And these tasks demand of us, in addition to wise judgment, a spirit of joyous abandonment to the Spirit of God. Look at the rock whence you were hewn and the quarry from which you were dug. Look at your father Abraham – yes, and here's the sequel to that text about Abraham. It comes from the Epistle to the Hebrews. Let this verse of scripture be our inspiration and guide in the years ahead: 'By faith, Abraham obeyed the summons to go out to a place he would eventually possess, and he set out not knowing whither he went.'

Acknowledgements

The author wishes to thank everyone who has helped in the production of this book, notably Father Charles Sutton, Sue Perry and Tim Stanley but also Sarah Brown, John Davenport, Philippa and Norman Drewett, Linda Hudson, Wendy Mortimer, Andrew Morgan M.B.E., Quita Morgan, Holly Shannon, Jessica Smith, Christopher Verity, the staff at Bristol Record Office and Bristol Central Library and Clara Hudson, Stephen Morris and all at Redcliffe Press.